BITCHING

BITCHING

Marion Meade

OPEN ROAD
INTEGRATED MEDIA
NEW YORK

ISBN 978-1-4976-3897-6

This edition published in 2014 by Open Road Integrated Media, Inc.
345 Hudson Street
New York, NY 10014
www.openroadmedia.com

FOREWORD

In the spring of 1970 rebellion was in the air, and I—a freelance writer, wife, and mother of a two-year-old daughter—went searching for the revolution. But joining one of the activist groups that called itself the Women's Liberation Movement did not come easily, as it turned out. Redstockings, for instance, was not listed in the phone book. The National Organization for Women was. For several months I attended meetings in a church basement, with nicely-dressed women in mini-skirts and listened to sober speeches about equal pay for equal work. NOW struck me as too timid, however. What I regarded as more appropriately bellicose was the New York Radical Feminists, with its studious hippies and unfussy neighborhood brigades. While trying to locate the group, I kept busy attending the Congress to Unite Women, reading all the clunky feminist journals, joining a sit-in at the *Ladies' Home Journal* offices.

Then, one night in June, I found myself in a living room on Manhattan's Upper West Side. Ten or so women settled themselves in a rough circle. Then we began going around the room, each of us looking back and reporting on some experience from our lives, the ones that struck us as demeaning, unfair, or just plain enraging. Bearing a large quantity of suppressed rage, I felt right at home. I observed that these strangers were not going to judge, argue, or challenge. There was no discussion either. When one person finished, the next would begin speaking on the designated topic. As I soon learned, there was a name for this method of sharing experiences. Consciousness-raising, it was called. It could be loud, scary, savage, and vulgar, but never boring and always heartfelt.

Each Tuesday night that scorching summer I would leave my baby with a sitter or my husband and go off to somebody's apartment. Each week the women went around the room. Yes, there was plenty of bitterness, along with a surprising amount of laughter (which was of course often bitchy). *Time* magazine, in August, featured a cover story on "Women's Lib" and Kate Millett whose book *Sexual Politics* had become a best-seller. The author, as *Time* put it, was "a brilliant misfit in a man's world."

Man's world indeed.

That year 1970 brought forth eruptions of female protest, both political and personal, as women served notice that they would not play by male rules anymore. It seemed that everywhere I went women were eager to talk about their experiences. They complained, moaned, cursed, laughed, and cried. Memories without end began to unroll.

It was a time for slogans.

The personal is political, we said.

Sisterhood is powerful, insisted another slogan.

What should be done about men? Could they be educated, perhaps rehabilitated? Should hard-core resisters of reform be treated like kulaks, enemies of the revolution relegated to the dustbin of history?

Shortly thereafter, I began to record some of the acid conversations I was hearing. A few of the women considered themselves feminists, but most did not. No matter because the streams of discontent sounded pretty much the same. Their ages ranged from around 5 to mid-80s. They were children, students, unmarried women, wives, divorcees, widows, all of them major-league complainers about crummy jobs, failed relationships, frustrated ambitions, wasted lives. Most moving were the elderly women, who looked back with supersad rancor:

"What has bothered me," remarked a widow in her 70s, "is that everything exciting was off-limits. It was like window-shopping, strolling by and looking and your mouth watering but you could never stop and buy anything. Oftentimes I think my whole life has been spent just passing by."

Bitching was published in 1973.

The response to my book was predictable: it was not

exactly popular with men, or with those women who claimed to be satisfied with the status quo.

Transformation of society does not come easily. Yet it did come, and sooner than we could have imagined. Some 40 years later, we live in quite a different world, not yet scrubbed of sexism by any means but considerably altered.

What became of these women who spilled their grievances so freely? They went on to teach school, open restaurants, make films, see patients. Some are mothers and grandmothers, others struggle with the uncertainties of age, poor health, and savings depleted by inflation. A couple are deceased now.

Bitching is a woman's book: biography plus history plus memoir. Here are the life stories of a few dozen women and the way they were before Women's Liberation.

Marion Meade
June 2011
New York City

FOR LITTLE DARLING
who has the good sense to deny everything

TO MANKIND, WITH LOVE

> *The sun splashed liberal gold through the foliage, over the red cement floor, and over the ladies. They had been here since lunchtime, and would remain until sunset, talking, talking incessantly, their tongues mercifully let off the leash.*
>
> Doris Lessing, "Martha Quest"

When women get together, they talk about all sorts of things, but their juiciest topic is, and always has been, men. Unlike the male sex, women have few problems confiding in each other about their intimate relationships. They habitually spill their inner feelings. Over the back fence, on the telephone, in kaffeeklatsches, at the beauty parlor, in official and unofficial consciousness-raising sessions, women spit out their troubles, bitches, experiences, and rage. They speak about how to con, conquer, and above all, simply exist in the same world with men.

The current resurgence of feminism has made woman-talk a more profound and perilous pastime than ever because once a woman begins to question her own life, the next person she automatically starts to challenge is the male chauvinist nearest and dearest.

Women disclose their deepest thoughts about men to other women because:

1. They're not as emotionally constipated as men.
2. Misery needs company.
3. Who else have they got to talk to? Surely not men.

Men have never had the fuzziest idea of what women are all about. Or what it's like to be a woman. Or what women really think. Mostly, this is because they're afraid to ask. They suspect that if they do find out, it's not something they'd appreciate hearing. And they are absolutely correct. It is far safer to assume that women are inherently mysterious persons who desire only petting and idolatry, or to coyly speculate, as Freud did, "What do women want?"

But God knows men are not entirely to blame. Womankind learned early on to shut up around them. The shrewd woman knows better than to fully reveal her true feelings on important matters. From experience, she knows that candor is *not* the best policy, that it, in fact, can be fatal. For a woman, honesty toward a man is a luxury to be indulged in only in time of stress, or when she no longer wants the man, or when he already has one foot out the door. That's why, after a relationship breaks up, it's invariably the man who complains what a bitch his beloved turned out to be once she showed her true colors. One reason Women's Liberation petrifies men is that, for the first time in their lives, they are hearing women say *publicly* exactly the things they've been revealing to each other *privately* for centuries.

Since women have always found it impossible to be frank with men, they have subsisted by playing games. Not fun-and-games games, but serious games of sexual politics which are nothing less than a means of survival. From the beginning, women recognized that male supremacy is baloney. At the same time, they understood the dangers of coming right out and saying so. In their daily confrontations and skirmishes with men, they get along by playing woman-man games which, though they may amount to guerrilla tactics, have proved effective nonetheless. By this point, the survival devices are so ingrained in female behavior that women often are unaware of them. Although they may seem to play instinctively, gameswomanship is learned. If they don't figure out the rules for themselves, there are plenty of how-to sources, beginning with mother.

Men are forever squawking about how "women talk too much." At the sound of female voices in groups, they tend to fidget and then flee, dropping shrill, terrified remarks as they go. They have stereotyped women as chatterboxes, natural-born babblers of trivia, nits who have nothing better to do than sit around and bitch. Okay, fellas, right you are. But bitching as they gleefully remove the imperial male chauvinist's clothing is what saves their collective sanity. Bitching and game playing with the men in our lives is how women make it from cradle to coffin.

Admittedly, bad-mouthing men can grow wearisome, even for those women with no other means of alleviating their frustration. Furthermore, bitching is basically unproductive, because alone, it generally fails to alter the conditions women find so unbearable. A question women keep asking themselves is, Why do we tolerate mortifying treatment by men? There's no point in denying that they put up with a lifelong cavalcade of indignities; there's also no point in denying that they haven't any choice. As a sex, women are coerced into existing inside man-made straitjackets designed to keep them in a state of economic, intellectual, and psychological atrophy. Accordingly, women embalm their feelings and aspirations as they make the obligatory accommodations for survival in a world which belongs, implausibly, to men. The woman impolite enough to reject male dominance, whether the man be father, employer, lover, or husband, can count on appropriate reprisals. The wages of revolt, and every woman becomes aware of it, is inevitably some sort of unpleasantness. It makes far more sense to learn, at as early an age as possible, the womanly art of shuffling with a smile. Outwardly, at least, we aim to please.

Among the traditional birthrights of the male sex has been the prerogative to define women by telling them how they must behave and what they must think, feel, and speak. Judging from some of their recent defensive comments on this subject, one might imagine it never occurred to men that their self-assigned roles as interpreters of women could be presumptuous. Or, that women might wish to speak for themselves.

A symphony of women's voices is heard in this book. While I have changed names and disguised circumstances to ensure anonymity, the people are real. All of them are women I know. It was unnecessary to seek out strangers or conduct interviews. Rather, I spoke with friends and family, taping their recollections and, in some instances, asking them to reproduce experiences with which I was already familiar. Their voices represent many ages: five-year-old pros full of sandbox nostalgia; scornful adolescents railing at their prepackaged futures; single women unleashing sardonic memoirs of the so-called superior sex; women speaking from inside an institution—the one known as marriage; battle-scarred divorcees bearing oral histories on the sexes; aging veterans armed with voluminous notes on endurance. They are ordinary women with commonplace experiences. Their voices sound amused, contemptuous, outraged, irreverent, unladylike, and, of course, bitchy. Rarely do women whine to each other; they save that melody for male ears.

I have often thought that if men could only eavesdrop on womantalk, they'd rush out to apply for ego transplants. I hope this book will hasten them on their way.

ONE

Her Heart Belongs to Daddy

I. PLAYPEN GAMES
- The Fine Art of Faking Out Father
- Family Fascism
- Sieg Heil, Daddy
- I Remember Mama

II. FLOWER CHILD GAMES
- Little Princess Power
- Sex and the Single Six-Year-Old
- Miss Muffet's Fantasies

III. PUBERTY GAMES
- The Making of a Girl
- The Wisdom of Keeping One's Legs Crossed and Mouth Shut

Her Heart Belongs to Daddy

Let's face it. The war between the sexes is rigged in man's favor from the very beginning. The scenario for Round One is brief:

A little girl studies family power politics, sizes up Mommy and Daddy, and draws two conclusions:

1. Mommy is a mess.
2. Daddy is a prince.

Moral: Hop on the winning team fast.

However, there's no reason for men to feel cocky. Little girls may not want to grow up like Mother but it's equally apparent that Daddy, while a prince, is also a sap. Because even though Mommy kneels in tribute to Our Father Who Art at the Office, behind his back she's subtly (or, as the case may be, not so subtly) giving him the honorable old middle finger. A girl feels justified in doing likewise, and so, with the realization that Daddy is ripe for a royal screwing, she embarks on a lifetime career of exploiting the old man in one way or another. Disillusioning, but there it is.

Think of this chapter as an opening chorus of rude and disrespectful sounds.

1. PLAYPEN GAMES

The Fine Art of Faking Out Father. The first human being a girl meets when she enters this world is a man: the obstetrician. As if she already understands that Baby, It's a Man's World, she greets this advance man from the male establishment with an appropriately symbolic gesture. She pees on him. So far, so good.

The second man she encounters is Daddy; that is, if he hasn't been detained, bonding with his cronies in a bar or passing out cigars. There are two important facts about Daddy that she will eventually discover: 1. He's disappointed because she should have been a boy. (Mother, too, may have wanted a son.) 2. He usually manages to overcome his gloom when reminded that, even though daughters may be second best, there are some compensations. His newly revised attitude toward the inferior specimen is best summed up in a greeting card which announces: CONGRATULATIONS ON YOUR BABY DAUGHTER and reassuringly points out:

Little girls are wonderful—
They're sweet and precious, too
And who should know that better
Than a happy pair like you!

In case this message isn't consolation enough, the card manufacturer helpfully reminds Daddy what he can expect from a female child. The poem:

WHAT IS A GIRL?
She's a bundle of sweetness and brightness and fun
The beauty of springtime, the warmth of the sun
She's Innocence covered with mud, sand, and soot
She's Motherhood dragging a doll by the foot
She's a composite picture of giggles and tears
Of tantrums, excitement, amusement and fears
A bundle of mischief and often a tease
A creature of moods not too easy to please
Who can capture your heart with her pixie-like grin
Or chatter and beg till your patience wears thin
But obedient, naughty, mischievous or coy
She's Mom's little Darling and Dad's pride and joy.

Of course, just like a woman: sweet, innocent, tearful, fearful, a tease, a creature of moods, coy, and wouldn't you know it, a chatterbox. Lulled into accepting this quaint, if wildly inaccurate image of his daughter, Daddy makes the mistake of treating her like a Little Darling. He will never know the true *her,* any more than he knows the real feelings of his wife. Score one for our side.

The tone of her relationship with Daddy virtually set for life, Little Darling can confidently proceed to manipulate him at will, unless one day she makes the deadly error of letting on what she really thinks of him. Nancy, a twenty-year-old college student and her father's favorite child, appraises Daddy:

> *Until about two years ago I felt my father was the most horrible person I'd known in my whole fucking life. I really hated him and I still have a lot of resentment and anger.*

About two years ago she left home. Since then, she has tried to limit their reunions to occasions when she needs money.

If painting women as hypocrites and deceivers of men from the moment of birth seems too black a portrait, it's simply a case of necessity being the mother of invention. To some degree at least, all women are forced to dissemble if they expect to coexist with men by meeting the man-made ground rules for female behavior. The more successfully Little Darling fakes out Father, the better she'll get along later on in a man's world. Her only other option is to turn around and climb back into a woman's world, Mama's womb.

Family Fascism. Armed with the knowledge that Daddy can be used, a girl learns her first lesson in female behavior when she observes the power struggle between Mother and Daddy. One of the revelations apparent from her ringside seat is that conjugal conflict is a fact of life. Hostilities may not always be waged out in the open, but trench warfare goes on continually.

For reasons still obscure to her, one parent hands down

commandments as if he were a local representative for the Almighty. (Wait until she hears about the real thing, that celebrated all-male triumvirate, The Father, The Son, and The Holy Ghost.) Daddy's list of Thou Shalts mainly concerns his status. It is his right to be Dominant, In Charge, Boss, and Head of Household—a precarious authority he nervously struggles to attain and then maintain by means of elementary fascism. Nancy remembers her father's nightly homecomings:

> *We'd be sitting there, talking and having a good time. When we'd hear the garage door open, which meant he was home, everybody would tense up and change what we had been saying. We'd ask each other, "Is he in a good mood or a bad mood?" Always, always there was this kind of dread. If he was angry, my mother would tell us, "Well, something happened at the office today and he's just taking it out on us."*
>
> *We had such sensors. Determining his moods and whims became a science.*

Whether or not Daddy is the only parent to provide Our Daily Bread, he still feels entitled to control. The crude propaganda he passes out is meant to reassure his family, but mainly himself, that domination is his due. He's bigger and stronger than Mother, isn't he? And smarter? Doesn't he drive the car? Pay the bills? All of which conveniently overlooks the unpleasant truth that his only claim to power rests on biological accident: He owns a penis. If he didn't, he'd be in the same position as Mommy, skimming the Monkey Ward catalogue and marveling at the latest toilet bowl cleaner.

The politics of the family, despite its lack of logic, doesn't take long to decipher. Daddy may act like a megalomaniac, but the real issue here is his unavailability. He simply is not part of a girl's daily existence. In her world the key person is Mother, who *is* available. For all Daddy's soliloquies about how hard he works, the office or store or wherever else he disappears to doesn't exist. She only sees that Mother, hustling between the stove and the A & P, holds the short end of the stick.

As for the agitprop she hears about males being smarter, this peculiar line of reasoning may confuse her for years to come. On the one hand, she can see that boys, despite their ordinary human abilities, seem to be treated as special people. On the other, this is a preposterous idea which she can refute by observing her brother or the boy next door. A mini-view of the sexes from Laurie, four, describing the boys in her nursery school class:

> *YUCK! Boys are stupid.*
>
> *Well, I like boys sometimes. I like Charlie because he gives me gum. Once he gave me nine pieces of bubble gum. But girls are nicer.*

While Daddy appears to possess extraordinary power, especially compared to Mother who usually behaves like a nitwit when he's home, his self-appointed title of Provider, Protector, and All-Round Responsibility-Taker is meaningless because, obviously, it's Mother who runs the house and takes care of her. Before long, she also stumbles across the ancient unwritten female code which says: Don't let him know who's the real boss. In the name of household peace, Mother keeps her trap shut and manages to yassuh her way from one wash day to the next by playing the wife's Number One game, Conspiracy. A girl recognizes that Mother's game-playing is far from irrelevant to the family plot. It *is* the plot. That she immediately acknowledges the seriousness of the game is apparent: She doesn't blow the whistle on Mama.

Meanwhile, television helps to convince her that Mother's conspiratorial games are hardly original; they are universal. To a child trying to check out the true relations between the sexes, the most educational program isn't "Sesame Street." More accurate information can be found on "The Flintstones" where those consummate castrators, Wilma and

Betty, sweetly outsmart their Neanderthal child-husbands. Admittedly, Fred Flintstone and Barney Rubble, strutting and blustering in the best machismo style, somewhat exaggerate Daddy's behavior. But the undermining tactics demonstrated by their wives are instantly recognizable as Mother's daily biography. When Laurie was three, she was amazed to learn that Fred Flintstone wasn't Pebbles' brother. Her critical comments a year later:

> *When I grow up, I want to be just like Wilma and Betty. They have so much fun.*

One reason "The Flintstones" delights a small girl is that Wilma and Betty have won the family power struggle. For them, Conspiracy is a lark.

A more sophisticated version of Conspiracy is available on "I Love Lucy." Plotting and executing the games is a full-time occupation for Lucy and Ethel who happen to be pros. The reruns of "I Love Lucy" add up to nothing less than a how-to documentary on the basic principles of sexual politics.

Manipulation is the only way to cope with a husband. If a girl needs further corroboration, there is always Grandma. True, the old woman may be reaching the age where she's getting careless about the finer points of sportswomanship. After thirty or forty years, the games pall and she may inadvertently slip into honesty. But when Grandma chooses to play, her form is exemplary, her style brilliant.

From all the women she observes, Little Darling learns and stockpiles both their secret attitudes toward men and their devious practices. She is inspired.

Sieg Heil, Daddy. Everyone remembers that wretch, Peter the Pumpkin Eater, who couldn't support his wife and locked her in a pumpkin shell. The nursery rhyme doesn't mention any children, probably because they had the good sense to leave home at the earliest opportunity.

For all those years Daddy spends polishing his impersonation of a superior being, he might save himself the trouble. Four portraits of Daddy from grown-up daughters who remember him as:

JACK THE RIPPER - Jo's father, an accomplished sadist, emigrated from Europe to become a successful American businessman.

> *My mother claims that when I was a little girl, he used to take me to the bakery every Sunday and shower me with food. He must have beaten me then but I don't remember. The earliest beatings I actually recall came later, when I was eight, because then I started asking my mother how she'd met my father and why she married him. All she said was, "He was handsome." I gather he looked like a young Robert Taylor.*
>
> *I can't remember the worst beating, there were so many. Any time I'd cry, he'd hit me. I learned never to show tears in front of him. Once when he hit me across the breasts, my mother literally flipped out. I went into the bathroom to look at the black welts and I was really terrified. That night he slipped a twenty-dollar bill under my door.*
>
> *He'd aim at the weirdest places—my breasts, my crotch, across my face. Always on the front. When he beat me, he called me bitch, whore—wait a minute, some of the words are hard to translate from——— to English—, cocktease. Later he'd apologize.*
>
> *The thing was, he'd pick fights and I really never knew what I'd done wrong.*

THE STRANGER FROM ANOTHER PLANET - Although Bonnie's father isn't exactly Superman, he does remain an unknown quantity.

> *I don't know him. From what I do know, I don't think he's the kind of man I would want for a father.*

I've often met men and thought, "Gee, I wish my father was like that." I have no respect for him.

Perhaps the reason I don't know him as a person is that I can't talk to him. No matter what I say, he gets very defensive because he's scared to death. Oh, he's quick to give me an answer, to prove how smart he is. But something has gone wrong in his head.

I have very deep discussions with my mother—I know her.

THE TIN WOODMAN - Mary Beth sees her father as a man without feelings.

What drove me crazy was that I could never actually talk to him. Recently we were at Lincoln Center and during the intermission he's talking about how much this product costs to make and how so-and-so will gross a million this year. I looked at him and said, "I don't give a shit. Tell me what's in your heart, what you're feeling."

He stared at me, astounded because I'd never dared speak to him like that before. "I'm not feeling anything," he answered. It was true. At that moment I realized he's never felt anything. At least he's never said anything personal to me.

I went to a shrink once who told me, "If you can't make it with your father, you'll never make it with any man." Oh my gawd....

JUST AN OLD-FASHIONED MISOGYNIST - Nancy's father left no doubts about his feelings.

My father gave me my middle name—Isabel—in honor of his mother who, to this day, I know he hates. Sometimes he says, "You're just like my mother. All the same. Bitches."

I Remember Mama. According to Freud, girls enter an Oedipal stage around the age of three when they regard mothers as poison and clearly favor their fathers. Within a few years, however, they prefer their mothers again. Presumably Freud devoted a modest amount of thought to this phenomenon. While his observations are correct as far as age goes, his insights are good for a laugh. As with all men theorizing about women, Freud wound up faking it. He had no idea why three-year-old girls behave as they do, a situation he might have remedied by staying home and changing a few diapers.

By the time a girl reaches "the Oedipal period," long before in most cases, she's had a chance to log in several years of mother-watching. Alternately impressed with Mother's breathtaking methods of wielding power and horrified by her self-abasing charades, a child reacts with a predictable backlash. If a three-year-old girl were able, she'd run away from home. As it is, she runs to the only other protector she knows, Daddy, who usually proves a snap to manage on those infrequent occasions when she sees him. That, however, is precisely the trouble: She doesn't know him intimately because he's hardly ever home. Thus her "Oedipal period" lasts just as long as it takes her to discover what Daddy is really like. Curbing her agitation and making the best of a rotten situation, she eventually turns back to Mother who, grotesque as she appears, is at least human. At four, Georgina visualized life without Mother:

> *That was when I first discovered the idea of death. I remember thinking that if either of my parents were to die, I hope it would be my father because I'd hate to be left alone with him. The thought which scared me was, "Who will protect me from him?"*

From the moment a woman bears her first child, gears click irreversibly in her head. Although she may continue to give a creditable imitation of her former self, never again will she be the same person. With the placenta goes freedom. Psychological as the burden of children may be at times, she carries it even after they grow up and leave her. In the process, she emerges as damaged goods. However much she loves her children, no matter how completely she accepts motherhood, she's no longer herself. Instead, she sees a stranger who screeches drill squad orders. "Put on your shoes!" "Eat the soup while it's hot!" "Don't kick Jessica!"

If a woman is lucky, eventually she may learn to enjoy the daily litany of orders. At last, and probably for the only time in her life, she's in a position of real authority. Why not make the most of it? The woman who adapts in this manner is the one most distraught when her children leave, not because she's necessarily a devoted mother, but simply because her legitimate power trip is over.

To her daughters, she rarely resembles Mother Goose and she's certainly not the fairy godmother. She's the witch.

No girl wants to be like Mother. Bonnie knew it, and she also realized something else. Motherhood can drive a woman crazy:

> *When you're a young girl, you identify with your mother and I was always scared I'd be like her.*
>
> *Recently I told her about a man I was dating and I mentioned he was brilliant but he didn't satisfy me sexually. What I really was saying was, "I'm not like you."*
>
> *My mother stopped having sex with my father many years ago. When I was a teen-ager, she told me all about her sex life, which really fucked me up because I had problems of my own then. Her story was that my father didn't satisfy her because his penis wasn't long enough. If she'd had any brains, she would know that size has nothing to do with it.*
>
> *She wanted to be a little girl again. One way was to cut out sex with my father. When I was very young, she had a couple of nervous breakdowns because she couldn't assume the responsibility of*

children. Every once in a while, she'd get away from it all by having a breakdown. I remember her being away, off at———Hospital or some other country club. Of course, she was sick and very depressed. But when I got older, I resented it. I was left home with my brother and sister to do the cooking and cleaning and all that crap.

Mary Beth also thinks of her mother as a child, in this case an alcoholic child:

Everybody in the family put her down. My father first, the children followed. She didn't complain because he gave her everything she wanted. This was his way of pacifying her so that he could be left alone. When I was a child, he was remote as a father and I'm sure just as inaccessible as a husband. Often he went away on trips but even when he was home, he would be somewhere else. In the bedroom, in the den, not available.

Last Thanksgiving I went to his room and said, "You know, your wife"—I deliberately said wife—"is a drunk." He refuses to recognize her alcohol problem. He assumes her life is over. She drinks and eats and never leaves the house. She's fat, unhappy, and impossible to live with. And that's a happy marriage.

As the first child in the family, she was extremely jealous of her children. No wonder it's taken me a hundred years of analysis to straighten out my life.

A girl's dual attitude about her mother perches on the tip of her tongue. Penny, three, expressed it in one breath, three sentences:

I love my mommy. She's my best friend. She's a dumb bunny.

For a woman's daughter, the dumb bunny image is never totally eradicated (she puts up with Daddy, doesn't she?) but it may fade as she increases her understanding of what it means to be female. Like Jo, she may feel compassion:

> *As far back as I can remember, I wanted her to divorce him. Their marriage must have soured very quickly because I can't recall a peaceful moment in their relationship. There was continual yelling and fighting. While she acted hard and stoic, she constantly talked back to him and told him where to go. They never slept in the same bed and, later on, not even in the same room.*
>
> *He was always trying to impress her with the fact that she'd married an important man, a captain of industry. He came to this country to become a millionaire and build an empire. Naturally he wanted sons. After their first child, a son, she wanted to quit. He wanted more sons. To this day my mother says she never wanted to have me and my two sisters. I strongly suspect that her last three pregnancies were the results of rape.*

In the end, the message is clear enough: Mother is a girl's best friend, if only because she's the source of knowledge which truly counts. Take Sandy's mother and her "ultimate threat":

> *All sorts of games went on in my family and I learned them all from Mother. She taught me that you don't ask your father any questions when he comes home, not until he eats. Especially if you want something, wait until after dinner or he'll be in a terrible mood. That's what she did. She knew exactly how to get around him; her ultimate threat was not to fuck him which, she said, was his biggest fear.*

Mother's ultimate threat, although impractical for a child, is nevertheless good to know about. Little Darling will look into it later.

II. FLOWER CHILD GAMES

Little Princess Power. At the outset, duping Daddy requires minimal effort. However, by the time Little Darling reaches five or six, the old man often ceases to be an automatic pushover, a development which requires her to advance to more sophisticated techniques. Fortunately, her skill at scheming has reached new plateaus.

About this time, further complications may arise. Mother, for instance. It's one matter to study her rudimentary training tactics; it's quite another to put them into practice when Mother, Librium-hooked though she may be, is looking over her shoulder. What's worse, occasionally a zealous girl forgets herself and attempts to pull the same wheedling tricks on Mother who is not *that* big a dumb bunny. Renee's dissection of her four-year-old daughter Jennifer's behavior toward her father is offered with a certain amount of admiration for the child's poise:

> *She wraps Norman around her little finger. She'll say, "You're my sweetie pie, you're my darling." Once I overheard her telling him, "Let's go away and leave Mommy home." It's cute how she's always caressing him.*
>
> *It's amazing but she knows exactly how to get to him. If I say she can't have something, she pesters him until he gives in. When we were vacationing, she saw a doll. "No," I told her, "it's too expensive." What a number she pulled with Norman, crying, kissing him, calling him "sugar," and boohooing "I want it." She got the doll. I'm fully aware of how she finagles him but I don't know if* he *always is.*

When you're four, crying can get you a Suzy Homemaker stove, among other things that make life worthwhile. But as time goes by, the crude device of tears must be discarded. Betsy, a multi-talented child, found more productive ways to sway Daddy:

> *I forget why he wouldn't let me go swimming. Perhaps he just didn't want to drive me but anyway, he said no and went back to reading the paper. I sat down at the piano and played "Song of India." I didn't know half the right notes but I bluffed my way with such emotion that I made tears come to his eyes.*
>
> *I went swimming.*
>
> *This always worked.*

Little Princess Power is most effective when:

1. Mother is a magnificent teacher or
2. A girl is a quick study.

Some girls, Bonnie for one, are not:

> *I didn't know how to approach my father. He was always too busy reading the paper or he simply didn't want to be bothered. It was different when I was sick because then he always read me stories.*
>
> *I guess I was afraid of him, partly because he didn't talk. I'd ask him for something and he'd say, "I'm reading the paper."*

Interesting how it's always fathers, never mothers, who we remember reading newspapers. While Daddy was relaxing, keeping up with the times as befits a well-informed householder, where was Mother? Cooking her good husband's dinner, stirring his martini, keeping the kids out of his hair. After all, Daddy had worked hard all day. He deserved a rest.

The first smartass to make that smug remark about a

woman's work never being done has got to have been some father reading the sports hieroglyphics on his wax tablet.

Sex and the Single Six-Year-Old. Victorian standards of female sexuality rule the small girl's world. Expected to be pure in thought and deed, she is forced to play a double game calling for her to:

1. Ignore the sexual idiocies of her parents.
2. Conceal her own sensuality.

Sex is one area where Mother usually feels inhibited about passing along hard information. If her sexual activity is limited to Daddy, she's busy avoiding him at bedtime. In this case, a girl can't help noticing how Mother suffers from some exotic condition which causes migraines shortly after dinner. On the other hand, if Mother has had the good sense to solve her sex problem extracurricularly, she can't risk her secret with a snoopy kid.

But regardless of which particular game is in progress, a girl is left with the same clear message: Daddy wants it, Mother doesn't. The truth, of course, is that Mother is probably sexually starved, but what with dinner to fix, she doesn't have time to cavort seductively among the Teflon pans. Daddy, fresh from an arduous day at the office, likes to give the impression that he wears a perpetual erection. When Sandy's father came home from work, he took off his pants and walked around in his shorts:

> *His game with my mother was to always leave one or two buttons open in the middle. All you could see in there was this darkness, this forbidding darkness. When he noticed me peeking, he'd get a big charge out of it.*

As for her own genitals, it's a struggle to take pride in them. If she doesn't learn at home that her equipment is considered inferior, there's always some little boy to tell her what's what Laurie, reporting on the day's news at nursery school:

> *Jerry said I have a yucky pussy.*

Such male chauvinist pigletry aside, she does not easily lose affection for her own body. Nor, contrary to old psychiatrists' tales, is she necessarily impressed with boys' penises. Often it's quite the opposite. Margery, a camp instructor, remembers a group of three-year-olds changing into bathing suits. The uncircumsized penis of one little boy caught the children's attention:

> *This called for some kind of comment on my part so I said, "Well, Benny certainly has a* fancy *penis." One of the girls had very long hair, waist length, but that day it was pulled up in a ponytail. Well, Eva looked at Benny's penis, and with the greatest disdain and a flip of her head, she announced, "I have a fancy ponytail."*

So much for Freudian folklore.

Daddy's penis? Not only is it larger than life, but to dismiss it so airily isn't possible with some Daddies. Five-year-old Rachel volunteered, apropos of nothing whatsoever, this critique:

> *My Daddy has the biggest, biggest penis in the world. Yeah. He told me. He's like a horse.*

One's own sexual feelings are a subject to be avoided with Daddy. As far as he's concerned, sons are entitled to masturbate, daughters aren't. Since his image of Little Darling as an innocent doesn't allow for such unladylike practices, a girl winds up casually implanting the idea that she lacks feeling between her navel and her knees. Nora, a divorcee with a seven-year-old daughter, describes her ex-husband's feeling about Andrea's masturbating:

> *She's always been discreet, usually doing it in bed or the bathtub, but she's never tried to hide it from me. From time to time, we talk about it.*
>
> *She's never been so open with Roy, even before we separated. Maybe she knows he's a prude.*
>
> *I've only mentioned her masturbation to him once. First he wouldn't believe me and then he got angry. What kind of a mother was I to permit her daughter to masturbate? He's incredibly stupid. I wanted to tell him that all little girls do it. So do big girls. But I don't like to start anything personal with him so I dropped the subject.*

Another excellent reason for soft-pedaling sexuality is simply that it's dangerous to be female, whatever the age. At one time or another, a girl can count on April's experience:

> *The first penis I ever saw, other than my father's, was on the subway. A man standing across from me shook this brown thing at me. I ran away, terrified.*

Hanging around is only courting trouble:

> *SEX OFFENDER'S CASTRATION CASE GIVEN TO DOCTORS TO INVESTIGATE*
>
> *DENVER, April 7, (AP)—The president of the Colorado Psychiatric Society, Dr. Jack O. Stoffel, has asked the State Medical Society for an official inquiry into the ethics of the medical decision that led to a castration operation.*
>
> *The operation, performed to modify behavior, has raised protests among psychiatrists in the state.*
>
> *The attorney for the patient, a habitual sex offender who was voluntarily castrated 3 1/2 months ago, said today that "castration took away this guy's problem."*
>
> *Norton Frickey, the lawyer, said the unidentified*

42-year-old man was awaiting trial on 14 counts of child molestation at the time of the operation.

"This guy's problem," according to his own testimony, inspired him to molest four hundred to five hundred girls under the age of twelve. Although the number of conquests sounds like typical male exaggeration, it's heartwarming to know that Colorado psychiatrists rallied around to protest the loss of his dick.

Considering the state of affairs in the outside world, it's better to stay indoors. Daddies, of course, are never dirty old men. A girl has nothing to worry about on that score:

Even before I was six, there were sexual things going on between us. But the summer I was seven, I remember coming home one afternoon from the beach. You know how it is when you're hot and tired, so he suggested we take a shower together. I didn't want to but I didn't know how to get out of it. I was scared to death because I must have remembered something from an earlier age. Besides, I didn't want to see him without his clothes. My mother was busy in the kitchen but she probably wouldn't have said anything anyway.

When he was washing me, I remember being petrified and wanting to scream.

Miss Muffet's Fantasies. Misogyny is so respectable that a little twerp like W. C. Fields was able to base a career on woman-hating.

Man-hating, however, remains a no-no. The idea that a woman might actually dislike men is apparently such an unspeakable crime that there is no word for it in the English language. Besides, everybody knows that only a fanatic could hate men. When Valerie Solanas shot Andy Warhol, she was jailed on a charge of attempted murder and immediately labeled a man-hater by the press. Within a few days, however, she was transferred from jail to a Long Island funny farm. The fact that she had written an unsentimental analysis of the male sex, *The S.C.U.M. (Society for Cutting Up Men) Manifesto* probably helped.

While a woman almost has to be a lunatic to admit she hates men, a little girl can get away with such depravities as boy-hating. By the time a girl is three, she has identified the enemy and collected a backlog of experiences on which to base her boy-hating. But, like Miss Muffet who had been minding her own business when the spider came along, the little girl often avoids a confrontation. Instead, she fantasizes. Laurie again, with a bulletin on hostilities from the nursery school front:

> *Carl said he's going to cut me up with a knife and if I run away to the country, he'll follow me.*
>
> *Look at my muscles. I'm strong.*
>
> *I'm going to punch him in the face. Then I'll throw him in the fire and burn him up. Then I'll kick him out of school.*

Fortunately, boy-hating remarks fall into the category of Don't Kids Say the Cutest Things. A girl might as well make the most of a short-lived opportunity.

Brothers provide some of the most memorable reasons for boy-hating. Nora hardly ever mentions her brother's name without attaching the prefix, "that little asshole":

> *That little asshole Jimmy stabbed me in the chest with a pair of scissors when I was nine. I still have a scar between my breasts. I can't remember why he did it, or how badly he was punished. But if it had been up to me, I would have killed him.*
>
> *He hasn't changed. He's still an obnoxious little sadist. He should drop dead.*

With a little help from Daddy, a girl can easily reach the next step, borderline man-hating. Sometimes not so borderline. At the age of six, Kathleen came to a decision about men:

> *My father's habit was to stop in a neighborhood bar on his way home from work. My mother was always waiting dinner. If she was lucky, he'd pass out on the porch and she'd drag him in. That was cool because, when he could walk, he was mean. He'd be fighting drunk and often wind up hitting her.*
>
> *Once after he'd knocked her down on the kitchen floor, I knelt beside her and thought, "When I grow up, this is never going to happen to me. No man is going to get a chance to treat me this way."*

Jo dreamed of her father squirming behind bars:

> *When he hit me, I'd threaten to call the police. He laughed and said, "They'll never believe you." When I was older, I talked back and called him a bastard and a cocksucker. The last time he beat me, I was eighteen. I threw my knapsack out of the window and screamed, "I don't have to put up with you any more. I'm eighteen and I can walk out."*

She walked out, but she never called the police.

III. PUBERTY GAMES

The Making of a Girl. Years of Daddy-Polishing can give a girl an identity crisis. Who is she anyway—Little Darling or herself? Disaffected though she may be, still she grieves for the real her. Barbara wouldn't care to relive her girlhood:

> *The worst time of my life was when I was a girl. The problem was just that: I was a girl. And constantly being told I couldn't do things because I was a girl.*

The things a girl couldn't do, and usually still can't: bloody a few noses, climb trees without boys looking up her dress, muddy her Mary Janes, say "shit" in public, run away.

The things she could and can do: get out of mowing the lawn on grounds of physical delicacy, cry whenever she likes, preen before the mirror, avoid fighting her own battles by running to Mommy or Daddy for protection. When you're reared on Little Red Riding Hood, you don't think to defend yourself; you look for the nearest woodcutter. Even an adventurous girl like Dorothy needed the Wizard to engineer her escape.

At the same time a girl is concentrating on her Little Darling act, she also may be trying to satisfy Daddy in another way: by imitating the boy he wishes she had been. Georgina was lucky. She only got a boy's name:

> *My mother always told me, "Your father was mad as hell at me because he wanted a boy. That's why I named you Georgina."*
>
> *He wouldn't stand for any feminine wiles, which was unfortunate for me because a girl gets practice that way.*

Sandy became a reluctant tomboy:

> *I could never be me with my father. I had to be his son. The times I felt closest to him were when we were playing ball or washing the car.*

An echo from Bonnie:

> *I was first-born. So he bought me baseball bats and gloves, and a basketball. I became a tomboy because I felt it would please him.*

Roberta's father expected her to be both feminine and smart, a combination she found impossible:

> *The dominant factor in my relations with men has been that my mind and body are split. As early as first grade, I learned that doing well in school was very high on my father's list of priorities. Getting good grades meant he would love me. But at the same time it was very important to him that I be feminine and pretty. These two things didn't seem to go together.*
>
> *Ever since, when a man has made both of these demands on me simultaneously, I freak out.*

Confusion about Who Am I? solves itself. She's the unwanted sex, the girl with the yucky pussy, the fe-male. How does she know? Easy. She gets her first period—and she's back to playing Little Darling for all she's worth.

The Wisdom of Keeping One's Legs Crossed and Mouth Shut. The necessity for worshipping at Daddy's shrine while regularly offering token hails to the chief becomes a nuisance eventually. If ever she imagined Mother's games great fun, her years of checking out their validity have proved that dishonesty toward men is no joke. It's living theater.

As Sandy discovered by the age of twelve, Mother is the only reliable commentator on the state of world affairs:

> *My father called me Peanut when I was little. When I got my period, the nickname offended me. I wanted to be grown-up. I think it was my mother who suggested he call me Princess instead. Never for a minute did I think he meant the nickname. In fact, I never believed anything he said. The person I trusted was my mother who told me about the way the world was, the part of the world that was me and my family.*
>
> *The things she taught me about dealing with men were all true. The rest I picked up from my older sister.*

"The things" can be summarized quickly (the order makes no difference):

> Rule #1. Keep your legs crossed and
> Rule #2. Keep your mouth shut.

From the time a girl learns to walk, Mother is warning her about the etiquette of legs: A "lady" crosses them. However, Mother's real point, one which a girl soon confirms from personal experience, is that crotch-watching is a universal male trait. Conveniently for men, a "lady" wears a dress. If she objects to men peering up, down, and through it, she'd better cross her legs.

By puberty, a girl's legs are perpetually clamped. Thus penis-proofed, she has the illusion of safety at least. Along with Mother's unimpeachable information on tight legs is a second rule: tight lips. Keeping your mouth shut around men is imperative because they seem to suffer from a psychosomatic condition which causes them extreme anxiety at the sound of a natural female voice. A woman's voice should be soft, her remarks brief. Remember the woman who doesn't argue or judge in Bob Dylan's "Love Minus Zero/No Limit?" The one who "speaks like silence"? Like the man said, an ideal woman is a mute.

Somebody talking usually means that somebody is listening. For a person who thinks he knows everything, listening is a humiliating position. Men try to avoid it if they can. However, the paramount reason women pipe down around them is fear of revealing some disastrous truth. Such as what's really going on in their heads.

If Little Darling can apply these fundamentals, she's as ready as she'll ever be for the meat market known as high school.

TWO

If She's So Smart, Why Isn't She Married?

I. IQ GAMES
- Brains: Female vs Male
- The Pros and Cons of Playing Dumb

II. HIGH SCHOOL GAMES
- The Boyfriend
- Sex
- Confessions of Ex-Wallflowers
- Extracurricular Activities
- How to Select a Profession in One Easy Lesson

III. COLLEGIATE GAMES
- The College of One's Choice
- The Shopworn Virgin
- The Illegitimate Student

If She's So Smart, Why Isn't She Married?

During high school and college, men must sense that women are intelligent, in fact, that a considerable number are a hell of a lot smarter than they. This discovery may confirm previous suspicions. Its ominous implications for the future are undoubtedly disturbing, but as they soon realize, there is absolutely nothing to worry about. Although a few vocal females may respond to their adolescent claims of superior intelligence by telling them to shove it, naturally they vow to steer clear of that type.

For most women, open display of intelligence is only a temporary phase. The chief lesson our formal education system teaches women: Forget your brain, and if you can't forget it, camouflage it.

Since this is not easy, a lot of undercover bitching goes on.

I. IQ GAMES

Brains: Female vs Male. A girl is surprised when men ridicule the intelligence of her sex. She is even more surprised when she discovers they are mistaken. Years of being treated as a borderline moron or, at best, a precocious child, do not result in one hundred percent self-confidence. While privately Little Darling may conclude that other females are dumb (women wouldn't care to fly with a female pilot either), nonetheless, the slurs don't apply to herself. In the end, the one thing which convinces her that women aren't inferior is contact with men. She has only to compare her own intelligence with that of the men in her life to know who's a dummy.

In retrospect, first there's the man she's been leagues ahead of for years—Daddy. The fact that Jill's father is an attorney, a profession requiring a certain amount of mentality, fails to impress her:

> *He was the only one in the whole family to become a professional and everybody treats him like hot stuff. He's always handing out advice and solving the world's problems. What has never ceased to amaze me is that people actually listen to the pompous fool. He doesn't have enough brains to turn on the kitchen stove. When he wants a cup of coffee, he'll ask my mother.*
>
> *Before I'd marry a dope like him, I'd sooner die of old age.*

If Daddy's intelligence doesn't command respect, her male peers are even less highly regarded. In high school, Madeline had no illusions about the basketball player who became her steady boyfriend:

> *It was the cool thing to be going steady and eventually I found this tall, gawky basketball player who turned me on as much as anybody had ever done. I thought he was sexy but deep down I also knew he was kind of dumb. He certainly wasn't as smart as me. My parents worried I'd want to marry Brian. He wasn't Jewish.*
>
> *Their fears were ridiculous because I wasn't about to marry anyone so inferior.*

Such early insights into the comparative intelligence of the sexes are useful later in life—and a girl rarely forgets. In any case, there are constant reminders, as Georgina notes:

> *In high school I considered boys to be big, hulking dummies. I had no doubt I was as smart as any of them.*

Recently I was at a television studio watching the crew, all male, putting on a show and using this very complicated equipment. They reminded me of the boys in school because they were the same kind of dumb guys and yet, at the same time, I knew they were capable. I guess the distinction I'm making is between basic intelligence and the ability to make a good living. All of those men earn more money than I do, I'm sure of that.

Not only does Betsy scoff at the idea that men are smarter, but she's also a bit of a female chauvinist on the subject:

Men are much less intelligent than women. Look at the men in my office. Dummies, dummies, dummies. Look at my clients who are mostly men. Cretins. When I'm explaining something to them, I have to speak slowly and patiently, and spell it out to them like they were children. Even when they're not busy looking at my boobs, they still tend to miss what I'm saying.

Of course, intimate relationships with men are the most illuminating because the moment a man gets close to a woman, he automatically begins to represent himself as a working member of the intelligentsia. Cutting through his intellectual bullshit can be simple, but nonetheless infuriating. Linda describes the problem with Willy, a temporary roommate whose irrelevant abstractions she summarizes as:

... crap.

He just had to show me all he knew. So he went on and on, trying to snow me with obscure literary references. Since I hadn't bothered to retain all that garbage, he made me feel dumb and ill at ease. I felt stupid talking to him and finally I told him so.

"Well," he said, "we'll have to work on that."

Like he was the professor and I the pupil.

Nora disposes of her ex-husband's IQ in short order:

> *I'm sure one reason I married him was because he wasn't too bright. But I still had to pretend he knew everything. He was a great expert on just about anything I happened to be doing. For years I had to listen to him expound on subjects he knew nothing about. I'd sit there and think, "Shut up, you son of a bitch," but I never told him how fucking boring he was. I'm not that assertive with men. Something in me says, "Forget it and genuflect." Eventually I developed the knack of tuning him out.*

The Pros and Cons of Playing Dumb. Despite women's private reservations on male intelligence, there's no need to broadcast the news. Smothering our snickers, we uneasily slide into our dumb act each time we happen to meet a man who might feel threatened by an intelligent female. Since that just about covers the entire male sex, Playing Dumb is one of our most frequent games. For best results, it's combined with the classic game of Smiling, an all-purpose technique which women have employed successfully for uncountable millenia to cloak the fact that they play games with men.

When you're smiling and tongue-tied, the transition to impersonating a patsy is not terribly difficult. Already disguised for action, all that remains is to put on a boisterous display of good sportswomanship. While con games are one matter, shamelessly denying one's intelligence sounds like the worst sort of hypocrisy. Maybe so, but the real point here isn't *why* most women play dumb; the real point is what happens when they don't play dumb. What happens is, trouble. Salaaming to the mystique of male supremacy wards off a host of catastrophes, divorce to name only one.

Playing Dumb requires an enormous amount of technical skill because at the same time a woman is feigning stupidity, she is also called upon to exhibit brilliance in selected areas. A girl first learns to deal with this contradiction when she attempts to please Daddy. While Daddy can't conceive of taking the female mind seriously, still he cheers her on toward the honor roll. Roberta, now working on her Ph.D., was a brainy Little Darling:

> *My father always paid lip service to my intellectual achievements. "Wonderful!" he'd say explosively, "Wonderful!" Even now he brags about "My daughter, the scientist." Or, "My daughter is getting her Ph.D." Blah, blah, blah. It's good for his ego.*
>
> *But in real-life situations, uh-uh. He thinks of me as a woman. When all the family comes home for the holidays, he'll call my brothers upstairs to talk about property and insurance and wills. He would no more discuss those matters with me than the man in the moon. And I'm the oldest child. When he dies, who will become the head of the family? You can bet it won't be me.*

Another contradiction which bears looking into is the relationship between her parents. As a girl recognizes, Mother is clearly smarter, if her genius only lies in games which make a monkey out of Daddy. However, one of Daddy's more puzzling habits is affectionately demeaning his wife's intelligence in front of the kids. Every Daddy comes up with a couple of pet nicknames—"stupid," "dingbat," "fruitcake," to mention only a few—and every mother smiles indulgently, in front of the kids, that is. The fact that Mother tolerates Daddy's aspersions gives a girl food for thought for years to come.

Straightening out the situation takes even longer when Daddy proclaims himself a feminist sympathizer. Other men may need the security of marrying a dum-dum, but *he* has always preferred bright, capable women. The proof is his wife, a *magna cum laude* who he will certainly encourage to use her degree in economics once the children are grown. His wife is smart enough to graduate with honors but, more important, she's shrewd enough not to bring up the idea that *he* might be the one to take a fifteen-year sabbatical from his career. Just until the children are grown, of course.

To some men, intelligence in a woman is a highly desirable quality even though they treat it as window dressing. In fact, with most men it doesn't pay to act the total nitwit except in carefully preselected areas such as stock market investment, taxes, and furnace repair. Each wife chooses a few tasks to showcase her basic flightiness and hopes the man won't notice these are the crummy jobs she doesn't want to bother about.

Everything considered, a certain amount of female intelligence can be a highly marketable commodity. Catch 22 is that the woman cannot be smarter than any man with whom she has personal contact, from Daddy to the local butcher.

The disadvantages of Playing Dumb? None, except possibly loss of self-respect, which has never been considered a trait necessary for women anyway.

II. HIGH SCHOOL GAMES

The Boyfriend.

Don Quixote and Sancho Panza.

Damon and Pythias.

The Three Musketeers.

In both literature and real life, friends are men. Considering the precarious state of affairs between the sexes, it stands to reason that there's no such thing as a chum who's male, at least not when you're female. Adolescent boys are no exception.

Up to the age of twelve or thereabouts, a girl knows damn well that boys are a pain. Once she gets her period, however, precisely at the moment when she should be extra wary, suddenly she's expected to revise her opinion and play full-fledged games with them. Nothing less than her self-worth depends on convincing one of those undistinguished brats that she is adorable. Since high school is the hunting ground for a boyfriend, it's not surprising that Madeline's preparations included a new nose:

> *It was a big school with no yard. All the socializing took place in the halls which were literally meat racks. The first day I remember walking down the hall in a new sweater and a tight skirt. During the summer I'd had a nose job. The boys kept looking at me and I thought, "They're watching me. They think me attractive. Maybe some of them will like me."*

Although some males, Daddy for one, are known quantities, the romantic girl hopes that teen-age boys will be different. You never know.

Along with her regular classes, she attends a course which turns out to be the most crucial of all her studies: Introduction to the Male Ego. She finds the adolescent boy to be a chip off the old block, for he, too, has been monitoring Daddy for all those years. The instant he sprouts a few hairs on his chin, he's all set to gorge on the ego goodies due him as a member in good standing of the superior sex. The trouble is, he's not automatically bowled over by Little Darling's captivating routines the way Daddy is. A girl realizes she must settle down to hard work. Carol has invested several years in studying the boy ego. At sixteen, she's a cynic:

> *I'm told that guys have insecurities, too. I haven't noticed.*
>
> *When I was twelve, my mother forced me to go to Y dances where I would wonder about the guys I met. Suppose I had to ask one of them to dance? How would I choose?*
>
> *It wouldn't have been on the basis of looks because I didn't think boys were "cute." Only recently do I appreciate that some men are beautiful to look at. What appealed to me about guys a couple of years ago? Nothing.*

> *What really got me were the uglies who had convinced themselves they were Adonises. At least, that's the way they acted around girls. They were obnoxious, too.*

Since boys don't appreciate chattering women any more than grown men, a girl quickly masters Listening, a game which has been a critical success for centuries. A combination of Playing Dumb and Keeping One's Mouth Shut, it is best described as non-talk talking. Kathleen boned up on the basic rules:

> *I read* Seventeen *magazine and the books on how to get that boy and keep him. Everything I read said that my primary function was to be a good listener.*
>
> *"He loves to talk about himself."*
>
> *"Just keep him talking and he'll go on for hours."*
>
> *"You'll be amazed how bright he'll think you are if you can just keep him talking about himself."*
>
> *What a schmuck I was.*

When a girl puts Listening into practice, she finds that she's struck such a rich vein, it would be a shame not to mine it. Recognizing that capturing a boy's attention meant status, Sandy proceeded with zeal:

> *I developed a whole act for talking to boys. It was flirting, twisting my hips, but mostly listening to them talk about sports and cars. Never anything I really wanted to hear. Sometimes I'd let them put their arm around me. All that counted was that some guy was paying attention to me. What he said didn't really matter.*

Before a girl can execute Listening, she must draw the boy's attention away from sports and cars long enough to notice her. Although this is difficult, it's not impossible. Second to sports and cars on the male's list of interests is sex. Just as critical for a girl, then, is the necessity to swiftly transform herself into a sex object. Georgina was dying to try:

> *The boys' ideal seemed to be a girl who was small, petite, and shapely. I must have grown fast because in high school I was larger and taller than most boys. Even then, I had the feeling they wanted you to be smaller and lesser. I devoured articles on how to use makeup and wear clothes, and how to act around boys. But it never seemed to work for me. I couldn't get the hang of it.*

If a girl does manage to get the hang of it, her dexterity is rewarded with a boyfriend. Here's what Kathleen hooked when she was sixteen:

> *His name was Ronnie. I thought he was okay, a little chubby maybe but nice. Everybody was going steady and I finally manipulated him into giving me an ankle bracelet. Triumph!*
>
> *His idea of fun, however, was to park. For an hour and a half, I'd be bored out of my mind. We'd just pet. I never touched him because I was masquerading as a good Catholic girl. He'd touch my breasts, which are totally anesthetic, and then he'd work his hand over my sweater and pinch a tit. This was my cue to open my legs.*
>
> *Ronnie was kind of cute but his hands were ugly. He looked like he was wearing blown-up rubber gloves. Eventually he married a girl with the same name as mine.*

Sex. The only achievement which really counts in high school is popularity with boys. Traditionally, that has meant Dating, a pay-now-fly-later arrangement devised by men for their own benefit. Accordingly, the rules have been made simplistic enough so that any male, even the most inexperienced or dim-witted, can follow. Because even today it is still usually the male who initiates the game, calls the shots, and decides when time is up, the odds are heavily stacked in his favor. His only disadvantage, however, is that he must pay. Win a few, lose a few.

With practice, a woman can twist Dating to her own advantage. As games go, it potentially offers an ideal opportunity for all manner of freeloading. However (why deceive herself?) the teen-age girl lacks the experience to swindle properly. Not realizing how little is at stake, she applies herself to the situation with more effort than is necessary. Denise equated dates with tests:

> *When I was fourteen and fifteen, I would go out on Saturday nights. I used to scream and cry for two or three hours before I got dressed. By the time I'd leave the house, the bathroom and bedroom would be a shambles. I threw things from drawers and closets, scattered makeup and brushes and combs.*
>
> This *was the test. I could have been taking the bar exam and I wouldn't have had so much anxiety. Once a week I became an hysteric, that's how painful the test was. In some way I needed men and therefore I hated them for it. I knew I got them falsely. I didn't really want them.*

Dating means a girl's introduction to After You, an outlandish game which forever serves as a constant reminder that deep down men believe they're different from ordinary folk. From someone on our side, like his mother, a boy learns that a gentleman opens doors for "ladies." When a girl comes across a door-opener for the first time, she puts on a dandy display of frailty and waltzes through first. If she keeps her mouth shut, she can get through the rest of her life without opening a door or lifting anything heavier than a twenty-two-pound baby.

A date generally ends in the back seat of some Daddy's car. Kathleen charts a date with Ronnie to its inevitable finale:

> *We would have a date for the movie but before I left the house, I'd mentally check the evening's schedule. I'd think, "Okay, we get out of the show at eleven, then we'll eat until twelve. He'll drive me home and we'll sit in the car until one."*
>
> *I used to wonder if he'd shaved because, if not, it meant my skin would be irritated the next day. I'd also wonder if he would try to soul-kiss me. But what I was really thinking was, "What the fuck turns him on about necking?"*
>
> *To me, the idea of catching someone and trapping them in a car to get your rocks off is gruesome. And especially feeling entitled to feel somebody up just because you've bought them a hamburger and a milkshake.*

Although dating as an institution is less fashionable among teens these days, the dynamics of what is basically a sexual situation remains unchanged. Courtney, sixteen, says that she's one of the few virgins in her class. Experiences like the following may have something to do with it:

> *Sometimes I've been literally kidnapped. One guy took me to an absolutely desolate area of Astoria Park where nobody ever goes except muggers. Another time I wound up in the middle of a two-mile-wide parking lot under the Triboro Bridge on Rikers Island. I've been taken to these places and attacked. I feel totally powerless because it's always the guy's car.*
>
> *You have to rely on ... God.*

God, however, is not reliable at such times. If a girl plans to have sex, she does better to place her faith in a contraceptive manufacturer. Inserting a diaphragm in the middle of a parking lot requires practice. According to Carol—an amateur, as are most girls—she is left with the Pill if she's lucky, praying if she's not. Whatever happened to condoms? Gone with the winds of the Sexual Revolution.

> *The guys in my school don't like to wear rubbers. Most refuse to. They say it decreases their enjoyment. They'll use withdrawal or they expect the girl to provide contraception.*
>
> *I knew about the Pill a couple of years ago but I had no idea how to get it. I'd use rhythm or hope withdrawal would be effective. Now it's okay. I have a prescription.*

Confessions of Ex-Wallflowers. If a girl is fortunate, boys will decide she's a dog and ignore her. If she was born under an exceptionally lucky star, she may be able to make it through high school without dating or going steady. This means she avoids tedious hours of Listening, but best of all, she can completely bypass sexual contact with the hormone-ravaged teen-age boy and confine her eroticism to someone interesting. Like herself. In short, she's the most blessed of all girls, the wallflower. Barbara spent her high school years writing for the school paper and enjoying magnificent orgies with Mallomars. However, she did socialize occasionally:

> *I was a wallflower throughout my entire adolescence. But in eighth grade, I went to a lot of parties, usually in Helen's basement The big thing was Spin the Bottle. I'd wait in horror for the damn bottle to come around to me, which it always did sooner or later. Maybe it was my imagination but I always saw a look of loathing on the guy's face. His disgust was nothing compared to mine.*
>
> *Later on, I coped with parties by immediately appropriating the job of operating the record player.*

> *That was my excuse for not dancing. Of course nobody asked me anyway, which was a relief.*
>
> *In the summers we'd go to Whitestone Pool. If you were popular, a boy would pick you up and throw you in the pool. Nobody ever picked me up. I was too heavy. Thank God.*

Annabel, eighteen, was not particularly unhappy to be a wallflower if it meant avoiding incidents like the following. An elegy to a fourteen-year-old boy whose name she didn't catch:

> *At summer camp they had dances where the guys would line up on one side, the girls on the other. A girl put one shoe in the middle and then waited for a guy to pick it up. I will never forget this one boy who picked up my shoe and made a face, a disgusted face.*
>
> *I was incredibly humiliated. I hated him.*
>
> *What was his name? God only knows. He had a penis and two legs. He was a guy. The rest didn't matter.*

Only an extraordinarily perceptive girl welcomes being a wallflower at the time. Most don't realize their good fortune until years later.

Extracurricular Activities. Meanwhile, other activities are going on in school, ones of lesser importance to be sure, but they still require a girl's attention. Compared to her all- consuming investigation of mankind, subjects such as biology and history rate as positive bores.

Studies measuring the scholastic achievement of boys and girls show that girls do significantly better in the lower grades. By the time they reach high school, however, their grades range from so-so to fairly good. The only surprise about this data is that girls make out as well as they do. In fact, an enterprising female chauvinist might use this data as the basis of a case for the superior intelligence of women, because adolescent girls manage to perform adequately in class even though their minds are almost entirely elsewhere. For example:

> *BALTIMORE GIRL GIVES BIRTH IN HIGH SCHOOL DISPENSARY*
> *BALTIMORE (AP)—A student at Northern High School gave birth to a 7-pound, 14-ounce baby girl in the school's dispensary.*
> *"She had no idea she was pregnant," the principal told hospital officials later.*
> *The 16-year-old mother was described as a good student who had never missed a day of school.*

Pregnancy, of course, is a major distraction. Most girls need only cope with smaller ones. Nora's academic record in high school couldn't be beat. As the top student in her graduating class, she was offered scholarships to several universities. But when she remembers the month before graduation, a time which logically should have meant satisfaction over her accomplishments, she thinks of this:

> *The afternoon they announced who'd won the contest for May Queen and her court, I was in French class. I never expected to win. Only the prettiest girls won, the ones who were most popular with boys.*
>
> *Then why did I feel sick when I heard the winners' names? It was more than feeling sick; I was ashamed because I felt like a failure. That I was going to be valedictorian didn't matter a bit. The real honors were being passed out that day.*

Rivalry with other girls, over boys, remains the important competition. If a girl wants to compete academically, she runs the risk of succeeding and getting stuck with the label "brain."

To forestall any such calamity, she plays a two-pronged game, Underground Scholar, which runs roughly like this:

> 1. She competes without appearing to. Hopefully nobody will notice.
> 2. She hides any ambition for the future which does not involve men and babies.

In other words, she tries to act normal.

Since admitting she's a serious student would mean the kiss of death to her maneuvers to bag a boyfriend, she's not crazy enough to brag about good marks. If by some chance the word gets out, she poses as an innocent victim. It isn't her fault. Daddy expects her to go to college. In any case, she must convince the adolescent male establishment in general and a boyfriend in particular that academic achievements mean nothing to her. What's more, she surely doesn't imagine herself smarter than the boyfriend. Rarely is he difficult to convince. Madeline was able to make outstanding marks and still hang on to her basketball player throughout most of high school. Her intelligence, nicely disguised, wasn't the problem; his was:

> *After going steady two years, we finally happened to be in the same class. Chemistry. I always sat in front of him so that I could pretend he wasn't there.*
>
> *I wasn't much good in chemistry but I was better than he. I thought, "If chemistry is my weakest subject and I'm so much better than him, that has to mean he's pretty dumb." I hated him during those classes. I had to pretend he wasn't there because I had nothing but contempt for him. But the minute we'd leave the classroom, I'd be all turned on again. Even though I knew he was dumb, that didn't mean I didn't suffer and cry and wait for him to call me on the telephone.*

Avoiding competition with men is a habit not easily broken. Roberta regrets that she has never been able to have an intellectual relationship with a man with whom she was intimately involved:

> *My intellectual relationships have been with women. If I rack my brain, I can't recall having a truly intelligent conversation with a male who I considered a potential sex partner. The only exceptions have been men out of the realm of possibility because they were married to friends of mine.*
>
> *I didn't want to compete with men in any way. I suppose that's why I went to a women's college.*

In addition to the competition bluff, a girl soft-pedals her plans for what she'd like to do with her life because blabbing about her dreams is a sure means of unmasking herself. No sense wasting a good game.

How to Select a Profession in One Easy Lesson. Ask a little boy what he wants to be when he grows up and he might say a fireman or President. Ask a little girl and she might say a fireman or President. Before long, however, she catches on.

Even if nobody comes right out and howls, people tend to smile peculiarly. As soon as she learns to say "a mother," she finds out that she's not permitted to be a mother without a man. Finally, she arrives at the acceptable response, "I want to get married." This is an all-purpose statement which can be modified in case of emergency to, "I'm studying medicine but... I want to get married."

Up against the old male party line which declares anatomy to be destiny, she is pressured into selecting an occupation suitable for her sex. Translated, this mumbo-jumbo means the jobs men don't want, either because they're low-paying or because they involve children. The best clue to men's attitude toward children is that the largest number of male teachers are employed on the high school level. The number declines progressively until nursery school, where they are practically nonexistent. Even when men are paid, the idea of dealing with children scares them. If they had to care for kids without pay, coin-operated abortionmats would spring up on every corner.

Her preordained niche made clear, a girl feels foolish should she wish to reject such professions as typist, sales clerk, or secretary. When Felicia collided with Mr. Samuelson, she was seventeen and dreamed of becoming Someone, specifically Eugene O'Neill:

> *I wanted to be a playwright. It was more than a fantasy, I really thought I was a creative person who could write for the theater.*
>
> *The first male chauvinist pig I ever encountered was the guidance counselor in high school, Mr. Samuelson. When he wasn't telling people what they should do with their lives, he coached the basketball team. After I explained how I wanted to write plays, he said that was wonderful but had I considered how I would support myself?*
>
> *His advice was to learn typing and shorthand and find a job as a secretary. And while I was at it, I should keep my eye open for a husband. Then, after I'd done all that,* then *I could think about playwriting.*
>
> *The horrible part was, I took his advice. For a while anyway, I was a secretary. The reason I hated Mr. Samuelson was, he didn't think for a minute that my ambitions were important.*

Girls with an average amount of professional ambition wind up as teachers, nurses, or even writers which, if not a totally feminine occupation, still doesn't qualify as a proper job for a hairy-chested male.

The super-ambitious girl, the one who wanted to be President, has two options. Either she can aspire to be the wife of the President, a spoof ensuring applause on all sides because it is both feminine and patriotic, or she fools everybody completely by saying she plans to become an actress. Then she is free to persevere for years in a profession which demands the ambition and drive of a presidential hopeful. At the same time, she escapes the charge of unwomanly ambition. The reason so many young girls aspire to be actresses (or models or dancers) is, it's a grown-up version of Underground Scholar—seemingly effortless (everybody knows that acting requires no effort) plus rivalry with other women. And if a girl does happen to succeed, she can always explain it wasn't her doing. Somebody discovered her.

III. COLLEGIATE GAMES

The College of One's Choice. It's marriage, but that doesn't prevent a young woman from killing time in various institutions while she's waiting. If this sounds like a waste of Daddy's money, not to mention educational facilities, it's certainly not her fault. Why should she point out that the master sex is merely paying lip service to sexual equality?

Those colleges which admit women profess to believe they are serious students who eventually will apply their educations to some endeavor more stimulating than reading the directions on a Drano can. Admittedly, the schools know something the eighteen-year-old student would prefer to forget: She *will* use her education primarily to read the directions on a Drano can. Her hope, and the reason many women attend college in the first place, is to meet and marry a man with an earning potential high enough so that, in her old age at least, she can hire someone else to read Drano cans. (That someone else will be a woman who also hoped to marry a man with an earning potential, et cetera.)

The most successful college woman finds a husband and joins the legions of dropouts. Since she was never *in* to begin with, nobody particularly cares, not even Daddy, if the man is impressive enough. Instead, congratulations are extended all around. She's "a smart girl."

A woman with a gambling instinct searches for a pre-med student, but any man aiming higher than a B.A. will do. In exchange for the security of marriage on the spot, she volunteers to drop out, take a typist's job, and support him while he finishes his studies. After an investment of perhaps five or six years, she winds up with something really solid, a professional man whose income is high enough for her to hire a Drano can reader immediately. The risks, however, are well-known, because after five or six years he is just as likely to dump her. To forestall any such disaster, she wages an all-out brainwashing campaign to instill the proper gratitude. If she has misjudged his character and his potential for guilt, she indirectly gets her money back by demanding a sufficient amount of severance pay. Alimony is something the professional man can well afford. Either way, the smart woman comes out ahead.

However, the woman who's still hanging around at commencement is by no means a failure. Her college degree is a union card which qualifies her to become the domestic consort of a college-educated man. She has to hurry, though, because the card expires after a limited period, generally in the neighborhood of her thirtieth birthday, at which time she qualifies for sympathy.

The Shopworn Virgin. By the time a woman reaches college, she's tired. Provided she hasn't already lost her virginity behind a Howard Johnson's, she may decide to take advantage of the licentious academic atmosphere and get the business over with. She looks around to couple with a tender, sympathetic man who not only will appreciate the significance of her gesture but still respect her afterward. Rumors that such a man exists turn out to be unfounded. Indeed, to say that college men are insensitive would run the risk of overpraising them. Sooner or later then, she settles. Like Amy:

Getting invited to a college weekend at one of the Ivy League schools was a big status symbol. When I was a freshman, this guy invited me for a weekend at Dartmouth. On Saturday night we were supposed to go to a basketball game but instead he suggested we go to his room. I noticed that he locked the door.

Now, I was ready to give up my virginity because losing it was another status symbol. But I was also terrified. To let him know that I considered this a degrading experience, I said, "You keep your clothes on. I want to get undressed in front of you."

However, it was obvious he missed my point. He was too busy showing me his erection and saying, "Look how hard it is." Five seconds after I'd undressed, he had his clothes off. No foreplay was followed by a very fast intercourse. Afterward he got dressed and said, "I'm going to get something." I heard him lock the door from the outside.

A half hour later he returned with a package of Trojans and asked me to come downstairs where he'd built a fire in one of the main rooms of the fraternity house. I felt incredibly lonely; there was no one to rescue me. We got undressed again and lay down by the fire for seconds with the Trojans, when in walks a guy with a German shepherd. I didn't say a word because I knew from the movies that women aren't supposed to say anything during sex except, "Ah, ah, ah ..." But finally I said, "You could have locked the door."

The next morning I told him that I loved him. I went through the whole love routine because there was no other way to justify such a horrendous experience. At the train station, he handed me a bottle of yellow liquid: "I don't think anything happened but if it did, you'd better douche with this." He got it from the army. I never used the vile-looking crap.

> *I heard from him once afterward. He looked me up about three months later. I'm sure it was just to make sure I wasn't pregnant.*

The Sexual Revolution, a man-made insurrection which has set women back several centuries, forces young women in particular to become standard-bearers for the so-called new morality. Now that so many have been liberated, the competition these days makes it more difficult for a virgin to find a man to accommodate her. Eager for emancipation, Nancy had a run of false starts with jaded men:

> *I was desperate to lose my virginity. With whom wasn't important. I just wanted it over and done with.*
>
> *There did happen to be one guy who I adored. One night he got on top of me and said he wanted to make love. The problem was, Where? I thought the occasion demanded privacy, so I told him to wait until the next day and I'd get the key to a friend's room. I made all the arrangements and then waited for him to bring up the subject again. He never did.*
>
> *Another possibility was Billy. This time I went to Planned Parenthood and got the Pill. After hinting around, I finally had to confront him by asking if he would like to sleep with me. He said, "No." "All right," I said. "That's cool." For months after that, I didn't even hear from him.*
>
> *Finally I lost my virginity on New Year's Eve at my girl friend's house in Allentown. I met the guy that night and never saw him again.*

Once a woman realizes that sexual liberation only means cheerfully acquiescing to any man who asks her, the result may be a puritanical backlash. In Susan's case, sleeping around makes her wonder about men:

> *Sometimes I wonder how guys feel about themselves. I would like to ask them, "How do you feel about women? How do you feel about the women you fuck?"*
>
> *Because I don't think they'd dream of behaving like a woman. Would they lie on their backs and spread their legs for somebody they hardly knew? Without getting much gratification, only a modicum of attention?*
>
> *We all know what guys do when* they *aren't sexually satisfied. They have tantrums. They call you a cocktease. They make you feel despicable and guilty.*

Jo, a sophomore, solved the emancipation problem by retirement. A report from a twenty-year-old celibate:

> *From the start, I got fucked over by men. All of my sexual encounters were quickies. Finally I decided that wasn't for me and I quit. I like myself better now.*
>
> *Being celibate has made life easier. And frankly I need all the breaks I can get.*

The Illegitimate Student. It makes no difference whether a young woman matriculates to pursue a husband or a degree. Once she enters college, another institution dedicated to keeping the world safe for male supremacy, she's treated as a bastard scholar all the same. Since her ultimate academic achievement is failure, or at least avoiding success, it seems silly to sweat over her goal. Fortunately, colleges offer special curricula for those students whose future occupations will be figuring out the correct measurements for baby formulas. Guessing that women might balk at reading lists limited to Spock, Gesell, and Bettelheim, colleges schedule a wide variety of Minnie Mouse courses generally falling under the heading of liberal arts, a euphemism for nice but useless knowledge. Actually, liberal arts courses are not entirely worthless, since they qualify a woman to be an office housekeeper in such "glamour" fields as publishing and entertainment. Should she reject a profession where her chief function is saving some boss the trouble of slitting open his morning mail, liberal arts will still serve as an introduction to the housewife's self- improvement courses she will need later on: Passport to Music, Basic Crochet Workshop, and The Fundamentals of Chinese Bamboo Painting.

Of course if a woman doesn't mind getting caught flat-footed, she can always risk her femininity by preparing for a man's profession. The trouble is, she usually winds up voluntarily abandoning her "masculine" aspirations. Beverly found an inhospitable reception in a traditional male program:

> *I was an anthropology major until I discovered that only men got good jobs. One reason I wanted to go into this profession was to do field work. I was informed that, even if I got a doctor's degree, I wouldn't be permitted on expeditions unless I were married to another anthropologist. The men might find it inconvenient to have an unmarried woman along.*
>
> *Female anthropologists, or so I was told, worked in museums. Since the idea of spending my life in a museum was unappealing, I transferred to another program.*

Even if a woman is happy with the female educational ghetto, she finds that Minnie Mouse courses are taught by men who fail to appreciate the beauties of female aggression. She soon tumbles to the primary collegiate game, Male Chauvinist Pig Professor-Polishing, which is basically a composite of Keeping One's Mouth Shut and Listening. Georgina learned its principles by watching her sister students, but she herself decided to remain on the sidelines:

> *The girls who got along best in my classes were the ones who knew how to handle the professors. I'll never forget one girl who had previously been at Barnard. That school must teach their girls how to handle men because I've noticed they always do that kind of thing so well. Anyway, this girl followed the professor around and asked for jobs to do. She was also sweet, quiet, and unaggressive which he seemed to like very much. In her case, she had something extra going. Not only was she terribly quiet but she was also an orphan. During the war, she'd been in a concentration camp where she lost her parents. Her past life, plus the sweet way she looked up to the teacher, turned out to be an unbeatable combination.*
>
> *The message I got was that you had to sit at the professor's feet. For a time, I considered doing this and then decided against it.*

A jaundiced Little Darling is now ready to graduate with a degree in art history. If she entered college full of secret confidence that she possessed a good mind, possibly even brilliance, she exits in a far more sober mood. Funny, but for four years she could swear she was growing dumber and men were getting smarter. Easy come, easy go. Perhaps it's just as well, because she might have been tempted to tackle a serious life work, which would have demanded real thought and energy. That prospect fills her with untold anguish because then who would marry her? Worse yet, how could she put her family first if a profession came first? And, most ghastly, dare she risk her femininity for the dubious pleasure of being a "career" woman?

If she ever doubted the illegitimacy of her college studies, commencement offers persuasive, if unwitting, evidence. For Little Darling is awarded a *bachelor's* degree. A diploma for menfolk.

THREE

Paychecks Are a Girl's Best Friend

I. HIRING GAMES
- Help Wanted
- Interview Rituals

II. OFFICE GAMES
- The Boss
- The Company Man
- The Ovary People

III. EXECUTIVE GAMES
- Some of My Best Friends Are Men
- The Double Life of a Female Executive

IV. FRINGE BENEFIT GAMES
- The Free Lunch
- Office Affairs
- The Corporate Pervert

Paychecks Are a Girl's Best Friend

Men have always regarded the business world as their exclusive turf, a gentleman's preserve to be feverishly defended against the feminine peril. Women, as usual, tried to be splendid good sports. No longer. Now that a sizable number of us have also become members of the labor force, we've begun to remark upon the one-sidedness of the situation. Lately, a few troublemakers actually have bothered to count their pay envelopes and compare the contents to those of men. Here and there, a rambunctious mischief-maker has gone to the extreme of filing a complaint with the Equal Employment Opportunity Commission.

But for the most part, working women still observe the office proprieties and obediently toady along as if they were born yesterday. This means, for example, winking at such hocus-pocus as equal pay for equal work when we understand quite well that few women get jobs equal to men in the first place. Doubtless our basic mistake was admitting we were quick-witted enough to operate a typewriter. But that's our headache.

In the meantime we dream of the Monday morning when we'll be able to majestically pick our noses in our private offices while giving dictation to one of the boys from the typing pool. Otherwise, we try to spend as much time as possible gossiping in the john where we merrily emasculate every man in the company.

Here's the inside story on the male sex from the "ladies'" washroom.

I. HIRING GAMES

Help Wanted. A woman looking for a job automatically screens the want ads with a sexual Geiger counter. If Little

Darling lives in a city where the classified section is broken down into Male and Female, there's no problem. It takes a while longer with an androgynous system, but there is plenty of light humor to make the search bearable:

GALS/GUYS – Fee – Paid $125
TOUR GUIDES
Gd figure, attrac, personable for public contact

The employment situation for women everywhere is epitomized by a National Alliance of Businessmen ad:

GIVE A KID A JOB AND HELP MOLD A MAN.

For the kids who would rather not be molded into men, there remains the women's work which business reserves for the delicate, noncompetitive sex. Since our innate abilities presumably run to smiling, serving, mothering, attending to trivia, and making sure the garbage is taken out, and since most of us wind up doing those tasks eventually anyway, why shouldn't employers capitalize on our talents? Nor is there any pressing reason to reward us extravagantly, because it is well-known that women are perfectly happy to work for nothing. Name one housewife who draws a paycheck for her sixteen hour day. As for job titles, business has created special ones just for us: "assistant" and the ever-popular "gal friday."

Custom has shortened both of these to "girl" (as in "My girl will take care of it").

The rites of preparing for a job interview are comparable to getting ready for a date. It means whipping one's body into its most gorgeous shape because this is the first, and in some cases the only, part of you a company notices. No matter that the initial screening may be conducted by a woman; at some point a man is brought in to make the final inspection. At any rate, it's best to appear in costume. At twenty, Nadine selected the kind of job she wanted and then dressed to get it:

> *My aspiration was to be a receptionist without typing. All I wanted to do was sit there, smile charmingly, and say, "Hellloooo." I went to interviews perfectly attired in a cute dress, gloves and hat, a flawless makeup job, and a stylish hairdo. And I was charming.*
>
> *A furniture showroom hired me.*

Using some form of sex to get work is such standard procedure that few women think to object. Actually putting out, however, is not required as long as she remembers her place and sticks to feminine occupations. If she looks for work in a man's field, she'd better slip into her chastity belt before leaving home. For example, when a woman applies for a secretarial job, she doesn't quibble about a typing test: It required two interviews before Georgina, a film maker, fully understood the necessity for taking a "test":

> *I was planning a visit to Israel and I wanted to make a film while there. The Israeli Film Board suggested the person I should see was a producer who happened to be in town and staying at the Americana Hotel. So I made an appointment and went over. Before I could begin to tell him about my idea, he made it clear that he had other things on his mind. "What are you afraid of?" he kept asking. The idea of being seduced in the Americana on a job interview revolted me. However, I didn't want to offend him so we wrestled for a while. Finally he got mad. "Just try it," he said.*
>
> *He wasn't very attractive but then again I didn't find him repulsive either. One reason I refused was that I'd never seen any of his films. For all I knew, he could have been a lousy film maker. I didn't want to sleep with someone untalented.*
>
> *A few months later he was back in New York again and called to say he'd like to see me. In the interval I had made a point of seeing his films. While the plots*

seemed silly, the films were well-done and I'd been impressed. As I was waiting for the elevator in the lobby of the Americana, I remember feeling like a call girl. I went up for one reason: I wanted a job.

He wouldn't talk about business at all until the sex was taken care of. Finally I worked up the nerve to mention that I wanted to direct a film. "Oh," he says, "is that what you want? Well, you'll have to write a script" Further discussion was cut off because he had to get up early and he wanted to sleep. When I tried to tell him the plot, he said, "Write it and mail the script to me." He practically pushed me out the door.

The only access I had to this person was to go to bed with him. When I finally did send him my script, he replied that he was tied up but he'd get back to me. That was the last I heard from him.

Why didn't he hire a call girl? Because he was too cheap and besides, he must have gotten his kicks from women like me. Well, I didn't have to sleep with him, did I? Nobody forced me.

Interview Rituals. Job interviews require a woman to curb her impulses toward hilarity and give a convincing demonstration that she has mastered the game of Attrac, Gd Fig, Typ, which is a post-graduate version of Playing Dumb. Although the formula quickly becomes second nature, an applicant still must take care in checking the want ads to distinguish the right answers from the smartass answers. A flair for comic invention helps:

1. THE DEAD END AD

COLL GRAD - SOCIAL SERVICE - $6500
Attrac, well groomed, must like dealing w/people. Knl of typ, steno, stepping stone for greater things, 4 weeks vac.

Right Answer: "Yes, I do have a B.A. in sociology but my real interests are working with people and typing."
Smartass Answer: "Stepping stone to what greater things?"

2. THE MOTHER'S HELPER AD

EXECUTIVE SECRETARY - $7200
YOUR BOSS, THE MARKETING VICE PRESIDENT:
I need a poised person with executive secretarial background to assist me. As my right hand you will become involved in all phases of the business. You'll meet customers, many of them important business executives. You should be attractive, skilled, possess a professional attitude, and have an outgoing personality.

Right Answer: "I've always wanted to learn all about the alarm installation business."
Smartass Answer: "Big deal."

3. THE DOGGIE BAG AD

GAL/GUY FRIDAY - $75
TV PRODUCTION
Producer of children's TV shows needs right hand indiv to help keep his busy sched. Attrac, typ, steno. Attend premiere parties.

Right Answer: "Sure I can live on $75 a week. I have just myself to support."
Smartass Answer "Myself, my fur coat, and my therapist."

Once she has successfully reassured an employer that her life's ambition is to straddle a Smith-Corona Secretarial 300 or wet-nurse a marketing vice-president and, moreover, that she gratefully accepts doggie bags from premiere parties as partial salary, then the next step is parrying his snooping into her sexual activities. Should she be single, Big Daddy feels justified in grilling her about her matrimonial plans "because we invest a lot of money in training you gals and we like you to stick around for a while." Never mind the male trainee who scuttles off at the first sniff of a job paying $5 a week more; he's an ambitious fellow on his way up.

If she's married and childless, it's a company's prerogative to know her reproduction timetable. If she has children, she must cite some dire reason for abandoning them. To answer these questions, which are phrased in dainty personnelese, of course, a woman must come up with just the right false face. In Sandy's experience:

> *I learned very quickly that the first thing you do when you walk into an interview is lie.*

The particular lie is inconsequential, as long as she avoids such crass replies as:

> *"I don't plan to marry" (Company translation: lesbian)*
> *"I don't plan to have children." (Translation: freak)*
> *"Taking care of children all day drives me nuts." (Monster mother)*

In addition to Attrac, Gd Fig, Typ, she may throw in a few immortal classics such as Smiling and Keeping One's Legs Crossed—just in case. At long last, Little Darling finds herself in an office where she now discovers what Daddy was up to for all those years.

II. OFFICE GAMES

The Boss. Daddy may or may not have been a boss. But hearing him expound about his daily safaris into the business jungle, an epic which eventually took on the stature of Holy

Writ, probably gave Little Darling the impression he was a VIP. In any case, when she meets a boss in his native habitat for the first time, she immediately understands who Daddy was emulating. The resemblance between a household god and an office god is unmistakable.

Not, mind you, that she imagines The Boss will be as easily duped as Daddy. Not by a long shot. Still, it's tempting to see if the cherished games, embellished by a few sophisticated twists, might work. As it turns out, she needs every device she's learned to date. The Boss doesn't necessarily see her as a daughter, nor contrary to what she's heard, a wife. The woman he really expects in his office domain is Mother. Of course, some bosses want all three.

Once a woman catches on to the idea that The Boss is simply a homesick, motherless child, she unhesitatingly manufactures a brand-new game, Hush Lil Baby. Since The Boss is oblivious to anyone's needs but his own, all her relations with him boil down to one routine:

> Boss: "I want ..."
> Mother. "Yes, sir."
> Boss: "I want it NOW."
> Mother (jamming a pacifier in his mouth): "Hush, lil baby."

Tending to The Boss's "I wants" happens to be an excellent preparation for motherhood and most likely the only training she will get. He may be outrageously demanding or only mildly tyrannical, but if he doesn't get his way, she can anticipate pouts, whines, screams, and full-dress tantrums. She finds that the easiest response is pacification, meaning that she comes up with an adult version of a bottle, a change of diaper, a distracting toy. And just as a real mother ignores baby's excesses and keeps reminding herself that his wants must be respected because, after all, he is a little person, so must the office mother smile indulgently at The Boss's improbable behavior. Cigar-smoking, senile, pot-bellied show-off though he may be, he deserves a show of respect.

She obliges—in between her twenty daily trips to command central in the "ladies'" washroom where she regales the rebel troops with his latest antics.

It's true that The Boss makes demands on the men in his employ, but his approach is never quite so infantile, if only because they *are* males. It's only around women, whether mother, wife, or mistress, that a man regresses to a helpless titsucker.

Should Hush Lil Baby fail, a woman can always resort to an emergency game, Tears, a Big Bertha maneuver proven particularly suitable in business. The Tears game effectively confuses and routs the enemy in any setting, but at the office, that traditional stronghold of the unemotional male, weeping creates a glorious disruption much like the proverbial turd in the punch bowl. Nobody but a woman could be so gauche.

Mothers like to commiserate with each other by comparing notes on the toilet training progress of their offspring and by exchanging data on the various torments they must stoically endure. So do office mothers. Four snapshots of baby:

BLINKY - Kathleen's boss is the jittery type. He would be more nervous if he knew of her dedicated sabotage.

> *"Blinky" is how I refer to my* boss*—I use the word sarcastically because I don't have a boss. However Blinky thinks he's my boss. Anyway, when he talks to me he has this habit of blinking madly. He sits in his chair, blinks at me, and then spreads his legs open. Like a lot of men in high positions, he assumes the boss role toward women by leaning back in his chair and spreading his legs. I never know if I'm supposed to look at his crotch, comment, or what.*
>
> *I do my best to get him in trouble. If I'm caught, I fall back on playing a dumb female. For example, recently Blinky was trying to pull a fast one with the budget; he ordered me to get him*

some information from other departments in the organization. On each telephone call, I innocently spilled the beans about the deal he was attempting to finagle. Sure enough, within hours the treasurer was on the phone giving Blinky hell.

Since it was obviously I who'd foiled his plan, he called me into his office. "You've created quite a stir, Kathleen," he clucked.

"Gee," I said, "I had no idea it was confidential. You didn't mention I wasn't supposed to tell anybody. My goodness, I'm really terribly sorry."

THE UNDERTAKERS - Sandy's bosses were two novices who formed their own company. When their venture began to capsize, she waved helpfully:

Despite all their degrees and their supposed brilliance, they were absolutely stupid. They knew nothing about the communications industry.

They hired only women and then acted extremely threatened because we were *women. There were about ten of us, each with considerable experience in marketing, advertising, or television. It was plain to us that Merv and Jerry didn't know what they were doing. Did we tell them? Of course not. We'd politely suggest, "Why don't you do this?" or "You don't do that."*

No, they wouldn't hear of it. Wouldn't listen. "We have a plan," they'd say. Finally I realized what it was: to destroy the company.

Ultimately they succeeded.

THE MARQUIS DE SADE - Caroline's boss was a professional sales manager, an amateur sadist.

Even though I was an experienced executive secretary, he continually challenged my competency. He used every sick tactic, from complaining that I never did anything right, which made me feel like a stupid idiot, to threatening to fire me and then giving me another chance. I reached the point of feeling like jelly. I would go home and shake.

He spoke to others in the office nicely but, for me, he brought out his filthy language. Every word was "goddam," "shit," and "get me the fucking file."

He would ask me to do favors which weren't part of my job like, for example, writing letters to get his dumb kid into college. Funny, but on sixteen hundred letters I managed to leave the "h" out of Christopher. "Goddam you," he screamed, "you don't even know how to spell Christopher."

I felt like saying, "Goddam you, *Mr.____, how come a Jew names his son Christopher?" But I didn't.*

I was a scaredy-cat. I should have gone to the administrative office and said, "It's difficult to work with this man." But it wasn't easy to get a transfer on whim and I couldn't explain the truth. Who would have believed me? Because I needed the job badly then, I stuck it out, hoping he'd fire me so that I could collect unemployment. Finally I quit.

I still have fantasies of bumping into him on the street and saying sweetly, "Oh hello, Mr.____" and then running a knife clean through him.

He set me back a number of years in my development.

SUPERSCHMUCK - Jill's boss suffers from an occupational disease. He's infatuated with the grandeur of his own voice:

Listening to Superschmuck is like going under an anesthetic: I just slowly drift into oblivion.

Each Monday morning he calls me into his inner sanctum to discuss the projects he wants me to work on during the week. Except there's no discussion. For an hour and a half, he talks at *me. He sits on one side of this eight-foot desk, swiveling from side to side, sprinkling Sweet 'n Low into his tea, and poking dainty bites of buttered roll into his yap. I sit on the other side watching him eat.*

In a way, he's fascinating because he chews and talks without missing a beat. I try hard to concentrate on what he's saying but he's so incredibly boring. By now a lot of it sounds familiar because he gives virtually the same rap every week on how the company doesn't sell products, it sells service. Blah, blah.

After a while I give up on the sense of what he's saying and concentrate on making the appropriate responses, particularly to his infantile jokes. Sometimes I catch myself smiling a split second before the punch line but he never notices that I'm out of sync. The words just keep spilling out of his mouth and dribbling down over his double chin.

The tough part comes later when I get back to my office and try to remember what he wants me to do. Some Mondays it's almost impossible.

The Company Man. The first impression a woman gets when she enters an office is that the place has got to be chock full of certifiable degenerates. It's only a theory, no better or worse than most, but one that is soon proven correct.

A new company man is greeted with handshakes and treated as a co-worker who presumably is there in a professional capacity. A new company woman, oops girl, is treated to a lascivious inspection of her sexual equipment and welcomed as a sideshow thoughtfully supplied by management. The fact that she possesses skills or talent is discounted by the men who regard her, first and last, as a female. Naturally she hesitates to disillusion them. Like it said in the want ad, the company wants her to be Attrac, Gd Fig, Typ. The men in Betsy's office see a smiling, well-groomed blonde who somehow manages to do the same work they do. She sees no reason to inform them of her grand objective, namely becoming company president:

> *They're oblivious to the fact that I'm their equal in position, if not salary. Their main interest is my appearance, my sex life, and discussions about why am I sublimating with a career instead of getting married. When I arrive in the morning, they'll comment, "How delicious you look," or it's, "Betsy baby, you're yummy." Little do they know, I don't want to be yummy. I want to be in charge.*
>
> *There's this one no-talent guy. Slinky Sam, who oozes in and out of the office in his Brooks Brothers suits and diamond cufflinks. He thinks he's a movie star and that every secretary is dying to sleep with him. He's married of course. His favorite line is, "A pretty girl like you shouldn't have to work for a living." What a chauvinist!*
>
> *Once he told me, "I'll have my girl type this up." I said, "It must be nice having your fiancee work for you." But usually I'm a pillar of patience and Miss Goody Two Shoes rolled into one. My day will come.*

The Company Man acknowledges only other company men as his co-workers. And, technically, he's usually right. Most women never get a job equal to a man's. When Diane searches her employment history for a male colleague, she decides:

> *Nooooo, I can't remember ever having had a male coworker. Any place I worked I was a receptionist or a secretary. There were no men in those positions. I've always worked* for *men, never with them. Even the guys in the mail room acted as though they were above me.*

The men take precedent in Barbara's office. The women, or so it appears to Barbara, are invisible:

> *My office is an exclusive club, one that's closed to women. The men talk only to each other.*
>
> *For example, last week the printer came by. Since I'm the production person, his visit directly concerned me so I attended the meeting with the idea of contributing something. There were five men and myself sitting around the table. I kept trying to speak but nobody would listen. They had the conversation down at their end of the table. They were tossing stupid ideas back and forth, going through this bullshit business ritual that men do when they talk to each other. "That'll cost you two thousand dollars." "Well, I'll give you a thousand." All along, both sides know they're going to settle on fifteen hundred dollars. To get their attention, I had to sound shrill. Because as far as they're concerned, I'm invisible.*

Invisible yes; inconspicuous no. Despite The Company Man's inability to look at women as serious workers, he's not blind to their presence which he treats as a carnal coffee break to relieve the exhaustive memo scribbling, telephoning, martini drinking, and trips to his barber that occupy his day.

Women in their place, is his motto. And why not, because the typical Company Man would never reach his desk if it weren't for a missus who knows her place. His work day couldn't begin without a woman to fill his spreading tummy, make sure he has clean undies, and haul his body to the station. After deputizing his wife to look out for the homefront, he boards the 7:55 and settles down to read such erotic journals as *Business Week*. By the time he moseys into his office, its male ambience a refreshing change from home, he's ready to plunge into what he imagines the most important aspect of his life, namely, his work.

By noon, though, The Company Man grows restless.

It's time for a woman break. Disguised in his respectable dark suit, dark socks, and sober tie, he feels free to ogle shamelessly up and down the street on his way to lunch. During the afternoon, he periodically abandons his desk in search of female company. These sensual expeditions are limited to the more timid forms of lechery, such as addressing the receptionist as "pussycat" and fondling his secretary's shoulder as he gives her memos to type.

By five o'clock, he feels ready to swing, but, nine times out of ten, he goes home instead. The missus waits dinner only so long.

Invariably, The Company Man peeks out of the closet at Christmas when management provides a convenient cover so that he may indulge his fantasies. At holiday office parties, tradition and booze encourage him to do what he's been thinking about all year: cop a feel in the open. Since Little Darling expects to be felt, she's ready with Gotcha, a game which only can be described as magnificently unfair. She allows The Company Man to make as big a fool of himself as he wishes. When he shows up at the office Monday morning, Hart-Schaffner-and-Marxed again as a model businessman, he assumes she has forgotten his escapade. Little Darling, however, remembers every salacious detail which has been transmitted in manoseconds to the powder room where the data is added to his dossier. Seldom is the notation complimentary. Gwen's toast to the pass-maker:

> *Invariably he's the one who's least manly and least sexy. I'm not flattered because I see him for the desperate, frightened little schmuck he is. He just needs company. He's like the man who separates from his wife and immediately finds a girl to sleep with. He can't get along without his teddy bear.*

The Ovary People. Were a company woman to be caught off guard with her bare ambition showing, she would leave herself open to ridicule for her gall, not to mention charges of penis envy. Thus, regardless of her position, she protects herself by acting like a secretary. As she well knows, any woman reckless enough to answer a telephone is automatically presumed to be a secretary, no matter how exalted her actual title.

The Company Man, as helpless in the office as he is at home, needs a woman to look after him. If he can't locate an official secretary, any handy woman will do. Hiding behind the fable that a businessman's time is too valuable to be wasted, he takes it for granted that some female will keep him in orbit. The straight-faced company woman becomes a virtuoso at Gofer, a game which calls for her to go for coffee, cigarettes, newspapers, and his wife's Christmas present. More important, she pretends to believe his pathetic story that he could certainly do these chores himself if only he weren't too busy. She knows for a fact that he's possibly incapable but more likely just plain lazy. It's a toss-up. Kathleen's analysis of the sexes at work shows a breakdown into the workers and the drones:

> *In my office there are two kinds of people: the Ovary People and the Testicle People. For some reason, having ovaries means you answer the telephone; having testicles means you don't. Ovary People go for coffee; Testicle People don't. Not only do the Testicle People make more money but they seem to feel they can define the Ovary People's jobs. As far as I can tell, the Testicle People do virtually nothing but carry papers from their desks to ours and say, "Here. Take care of this."*

The tricky part is *how* a woman takes care of things. Outwardly at least, she performs her duties with patience and good grace. A childlike smile doesn't hurt either. Mary Beth's behavior illustrates Little Darling at her finest:

> *On the job I play a role with men. Actually, it's the same role I play with men* off *the job. I'm a*

> *darling little sweetheart who's always smiling. Over the years, I've found that it has held me in good stead. When men at the office invite me out for lunch, I take along my lollipop. They like me because I don't threaten them. They can see there's not the tiniest bit of aggression in me. It's just like that when I play tennis with a man. I've learned that even if he's clearly inferior, I'd better not win. If I win one point, then I make sure I lose two.*
>
> *When I'm in my wheelchair, am I still going to be playing the little girl because it's too much responsibility to be a woman? It's quite possible because, unfortunately, playing a little girl* works.

A little girl can also get away with an occasional bit of sass, as Barbara discovered:

> *Certainly it's possible to talk back to men in the office. Quite often, I've noticed they don't mind a bit because they think of me as a ferocious, six-week-old kitten who is powerless to do anything. Justifiable anger is dismissed as vexatious ranting. They'll smirk, "Oh, Barbara must be having her period."*

Which brings us to the favorite office game, Menstruation, a foolproof ruse which excuses any uppity behavior a woman may indulge in when she's had it. Menstruation can be played at any time of the month:

> *Miss Gofer: You can shove the rest of these letters up your ass, sir. It's 6:30.*
> *Company Man: So it is. I hadn't noticed. ("Probably having her period.")*

Menstruation provides an opportunity for all manner of insubordination. That's why a woman can afford to overlook the daily tantrums of The Company Man who obviously suffers from a tempestuous hormonal imbalance. As Nora understates the matter:

Men have their periods all month long.

III. EXECUTIVE GAMES

Some of My Best Friends Are Men. The woman who plays the game of Attrac, Gd Fig, Typ plods along all her employed life taking orders from men. Small wonder she looks forward to marriage as an escape because even though it still means taking orders from a man, at least she'll have a sublime chance to retaliate. She drops out with pardonable relief.

The woman who not only stays but aims to become an executive is unusual. The woman who reaches the top with her ego and central nervous system intact is even rarer. Every step forward is made with the certainty that she's not wanted. In the beginning, however, she isn't sure. Angela recalls her initial efforts to get out of the glorified secretary class and into an administration job for which her B.S. supposedly had prepared her:

> *I registered at a number of employment agencies and waited. Nothing much happened. At first I wondered why they sent me out on so few interviews. It never occurred to me that being a woman had anything to do with it. Obviously, it was because I didn't qualify. I began to conclude that I simply lacked ability.*

By and by, she understands. How? Some man tells her. Nadine, a stockbroker, made the rounds of the brokerage houses:

> *They'd look at my qualifications and say, "We want a man for the job." Most of the time I didn't make a fuss because I hesitated to antagonize*

> *anyone. Finally, on one interview I got fed up and when the man said, "We want a man for the job," I asked him, "Don't you know that what you've just said is against the law?"*
>
> *He smiled at me patiently and repeated, "Well, dear, we want a man for the job."*
>
> *Companies wouldn't dare say, "We're not going to hire you because you're black." Or Jewish. But, if you're a woman, they come right out and tell you to your face.*

If she can overcome such heavy-handed bigotry, she may reach the summit of top management. The trouble is, she's the only woman up there. The rest of the inhabitants are men. Dusting off their code of chivalry, they try to conceal their hostility. When an advertising agency hired Nora as their first female television producer, she felt friendly vibrations:

> *The men paid an extravagant amount of attention to me. After all, the company had never had a lady producer before. At the beginning, they treated me like one of the boys, which I found extremely flattering. I began to act like one of the boys. Around that time, I recall telling my sister that I deliberately had few female friends. I had nothing in common with women, I explained, in fact my best friends were men.*
>
> *No kidding. I actually did consider some of the men in the office my best friends, to the extent that I confided in them as freely as I would have with a woman. All it got me were several bad experiences where I came close to being raped.*
>
> *Because I held a man's job, I found myself acting like a man: tough, businesslike, no-nonsense. It came as a shock to find out that the other women in the office, my secretary included, despised me. And yet I didn't dare act normal.*

The Double Life of a Female Executive: While she can live with the knowledge that her office sisters think her a cold, tough bitch, she resolves to give the men no reason to call her a castrating bitch. For if fawning is the staple game for the schlepper in the typing pool, then the woman manager is your compleat toady.

Already tainted with the negative stereotype that all successful women have got to be castrators, she spends much of her work day proving she's the exception. Positive proof would be revealing her true personality because, whatever it may be, a bit of the castrator would be bound to show. Her individuality, indeed any personal style she may possess, is the first thing to go. Cherished obscenities like "up yours" must be expunged from her vocabulary. Slammed doors, snarls, and tantrums—the hallmarks of temperamental genius in a male executive—are also out of the question.

God forbid the men in the office should get the impression that she considers herself their equal. Keeping a close watch on her voice for signs of stridency, she reaches into her bag of elementary games for Smiling, Listening, and Keeping One's Legs Crossed. Despite Gwen's executive title and $26,000 salary, she's second in command. Above her is Lyle:

> *A few weeks after he was hired, I realized he knew nothing. He'd pump me for advice on how to do his job. Obviously, I couldn't advise him directly. I had to slip it in, casually and subtly. I felt like saying, "Goddammit, why don't you face the fact that I'm more qualified than you?"*
>
> *He's constantly taking my ideas and passing them off as his own. "Oh Gwen," he'll say, "that idea is terrific, just terrific." Then he'll meet with the president and say, "Well, I've done this" or maybe "We've accomplished that." He never mentions my name. I'm always sweet about it when I really want to say, "Listen schmuck, don't take all the credit."*
>
> *Sometimes I'll tell him, "Lyle, I'd be awfully grateful if you would tell them I created this idea.*

> *I want them to know I'm working hard." He says okay but I don't trust him.*
>
> *Relying on me doesn't bother him a bit. His fantastic ego allows him to think of himself as a master, someone worthy to be in charge. It's his right to have someone like me around to do all the work. The only thing I don't do is give orders. That's his prerogative and he positively gets carried away. "Well now," he'll say in this prissy little cluck, "well now, Gwen, today I want you to contact so and so." To the secretaries, it's: "Cindy, now don't you go out to lunch without telling me. And Veronica dear, would you mind calling the deli for a buttered bialy—make sure it's butter and not margarine—and a black coffee with two sugars." He is outrageous.*
>
> *But I'm polite. I'm always polite.*

Sensitivity to male feelings means that she must play Superlady, a game which requires her to follow the script that says "Women are frail—treat them with deference." To help her remain in character, however, she must spend an inordinate amount of time and money. Her chief business expenses, not tax deductible, are the services of a hairdresser and an analyst. The latter, male naturally, listens to her beefs about the men in her office (the "ladies'" washroom is no longer a safe outlet) and supplies thrice-weekly tips on what a *real* women would do in her place. One sticky problem is how to deal with the horny Company Man who is now, of all things, her subordinate. Nadine describes her precarious position:

> *My job has two levels: the work I'm paid for and coping with the sexual feelings of the men I supervise. The men cause me a great deal of anxiety. Sometimes one of them will develop a crush. This doesn't mean admiration or respect, rather it's his way of dealing with a woman boss. One man told me, "When you come into my office, I want to jump up and see if my fly is unzipped."*

> *"My God," I thought to myself, "is that how he feels!" He makes me uncomfortable.*
>
> *I have to waste time figuring out what I'm going to do about people like him. How should I act and talk? Actually, all I really want to say is, "Let's work on this account, okay?"*
>
> *Whenever I must give an order to a man beneath me, I make a special point to sound sweet and easy-going. I'm always conscious of how I speak. Never would I dream of dropping something on a man's desk and saying, "Hey, Lenny, I need this by five."*

Hellbent on proving she's a real woman during office hours, she must do her femininity push-ups and tiptoe around the male ego after hours as well. Lovers are also on the lookout for signs that she may be sprouting balls. Nadine encountered two types of reactions from men with lesser jobs and/or lesser incomes:

> *Some men ignore the fact that I have a more important job. I can't begin to count the evenings I have listened to some guy talk endlessly about his work, his day, his hopes and ambitions. I say very little but I'm thinking, "My day has been so much more exciting but this twerp couldn't care less."*
>
> *Other men use me as a prestige symbol. Invariably they introduce me as, "Nadine the Stockbroker."*

In the end, of course, there is only one way to prove she's a *real* woman. She marries and, as soon as she can find a reliable housekeeper, produces three children.

IV. FRINGE BENEFIT GAMES

The Free Lunch. Considering the gap between male and female salaries, it's only fair that the male business establishment unwittingly underwrite the cost of our lunches.

If a woman plays her noon-time games skillfully, she often can extort a free lunch from some man in some company. Whether the man charges her meal to his expense account, takes it out of petty cash, or, failing those, pays for it out of his own pocket, at least the woman saves on her food bill.

Although the free lunch may be the most important company fringe benefit a woman gets, worse luck, it's not automatic. To qualify, she must first connect with Some Other Woman's Husband. This is the least of her worries because offices are full of married men looking for dates. Even though a man expects his wife to stop dating after the wedding, he merely transfers his womanizing from evening to midday and goes right on dating until retirement time. If his wife tires of eating yesterday's leftovers in between wash loads and meets a man for lunch, her actions are immediately suspect, which is why she generally doesn't parade the man into the most popular restaurant in town. Her husband, on the other hand, is safely covered by a traditional business practice known as "taking one of the kids in the office to lunch." Bad enough that business custom downgrades a woman into a girl; the free lunch further demotes her to a child.

Since married men are fond of spending their lunch hours in porno movie houses, a freelunchloader must nail one down before she can play Eat and Run, one of the safest of all sex games. Her object is to finagle Some Other Woman's Husband into taking her to:

1. an elegant restaurant. This means any establishment with more ambience than the corner coffee shop. Preferably one with printed matchbooks which can be exhibited later to the coven in the john.
2. a nice restaurant. This only means the corner coffee shop but now that Some Other Woman's Husband is paying, she can order the steak sandwich instead of the tuna fish sandwich. Every little bit helps.

Making the most of opportunity while it lasts, a smart woman concentrates on cadging a record number of elegant lunches. The day will soon arrive when she'll be home with her peanut butter and jelly sandwich while hers is the Some Other Woman's Husband who is treating a kid to lunch. In fact, after marriage, seldom will she see the inside of a decent restaurant at lunchtime, not with a man anyway and certainly not with her husband.

The easiest part of Eat and Run is ordering. Her objective is to stoke up so that it's not necessary to eat dinner that evening. Nor does running present any difficulty. Since men feel bashful about attacking women in restaurants, an approach can be cut off with a polite reminder that her dictaphone is waiting. The unpleasant features of Eat and Run develop during eating when it takes strong devotion to food and steady powers of concentration to enjoy what's on her plate. While she may be there for the *blanquette de veau*, Some Other Woman's Husband is not. If only vicariously, it's his chance to screw her which he does by talking dirty, questioning her about her hot-blooded boyfriends, and groping for her under the table; in fact, everything short of shelling out the money for a hotel room and doing things properly.

It's true, Eat and Run lacks suspense. On the other hand, should it end in sex, the game has been self-defeating. If a woman spends her lunch hour in bed, which might be classified as another fringe benefit, she obviously won't be able to eat. In the end, it's a matter of priorities.

Aside from Some Other Woman's Husband, the man who figures most prominently in a working woman's lunch hours is the male chauvinist waiter. This bloke never appears during a free lunch because she's with a man. He emerges when women eat together. Ordinarily, women dining with each other means ordering in, patronizing the company cafeteria, or making a quick foray to the cheapest place they can find. Few women would dream of spending $5 of their own money for lunch; if they did dream of it, they couldn't afford it.

However, there are special send-offs such as marriage and pregnancy which call for eating in style. The first person women diners meet is the maitre d', also a male chauvinist, who escorts them to the crummiest table at his disposal. The best tables he reserves for bonding businessmen; the second best for Some Other Woman's Husband and a kid; the worst for people least likely to complain. That's women.

Once their male chauvinist waiter is sure no men require his attention, he finds time for the "ladies." One cocktail gets his okay, two or three a display of horror, a request for the wine list his snickers. Since he can't imagine women have anything important to say, he eavesdrops openly while hustling them from one course to the next. Unlike his male customers, they request the check in soft, ladylike voices which allow him to fake a hearing problem and ignore them until he's good and ready. Unruffled, the women pretend they have received the same service as everybody else and collect their revenge at tip time. Protected by the assumption that only males excel at mathematics, they have no qualms about rewarding their male chauvinist pig with an improbable gratuity. But then everybody knows that women are notoriously poor tippers.

Office Affairs. Seldom are offices good spots to beat the bushes for a husband unless a woman is willing to settle for Some Other Woman's Husband. Undeniably, there can be advantages to marrying a divorced man because, thanks to his ex-wife, his chauvinism has been nicely weather-beaten.

In most cases, however, it's best to view the married man for what he is, no more and no less than an alternate source of free meals, free drinks, and free sex. If she does embark on an affair, she gets to play Three's Company. The first time she sleeps with a married man, there are two people in her bed (it's always her bed, a refreshing change from the grubby sheets on bachelor beds). But ever after, there's a third party. His wife. He reveals his obsession with her, second only to that with his mother, by delivering a recitation of the hellish indignities he suffers (The My Wife Doesn't Understand Me Syndrome).

Immediately, his description of the wife's diabolical schemes sounds familiar because a woman recognizes that they are none other than her mother's unforgettable routines. Mama, far from not appreciating Daddy, had him down pat. Already feeling a certain solidarity with the wife, she listens attentively to get the real lowdown on what kind of a man he is, while simultaneously offering sighs of sympathy for his afflictions.

Even more important, she picks up valuable tips for the future by learning how his mate plays one of the sexually-bored wife's chief survival games: Driving a Husband To Infidelity Without His Ever Suspecting. By the end of the affair she has an authentic blueprint of how a cuckolded wife makes the most of such a paradisiacal situation.

Although an affair with Some Other Woman's Husband can be illuminating, it has other advantages as well. Compared to the single man, with whom she is always struggling for the upper hand, the married man is far easier to manage:

1. She can keep him in a state of anxiety because he's never positive she won't spill the beans to his wife. (He'd be devastated to learn that his secret affair is yesterday's news to the gang in the "ladies'" washroom.)
2. She never has to make him breakfast.
3. She has the weekends free to Wella her hair.

So much for the plusses. There is one prominent drawback. Some Other Woman's Husband is invariably a miserable cheapskate. So long as he can charge the cost of her seduction to his expense account, she can feel reasonably confident of top-notch entertainment. Sooner or later, this is no longer wise and he falls back on his own finances, which may be closely supervised by his wife. The rise and fall of a credit card affair is detailed by Sara whose married man turned out to be typical. Over the course of their two-year liaison, he promised to buy her a typewriter and divorce his wife. Naturally he did neither:

> *At first it was champagne dinners at the Rainbow Room, the Persian Room, and every room in town. This lasted about a month.*
>
> *From there on in, it was beer and bologna sandwiches at my apartment.*
>
> *He never bought me a birthday present. He never bought me a Christmas present either, because he said he didn't believe in them. That I could accept. But the birthdays ... at that time I was making $90 a week. For his birthday I went to Tiffany's and bought him a lighter inscribed with our private joke, "Hiya Tiger." It took me months of budgeting and skipping lunches to pay for it. The second year I bought him a lounging robe with his initials.*
>
> *You know what his birthday presents to me were? At midnight we'd make love and he'd say, "Happy Birthday."*

Equally disillusioning was Mary Beth's office affair with Wendall, forty-five, married but separated. Part of the mistake was inviting him to move in:

> *In the office we touched sometimes and he appeared to be a warm, tender person. Later I realized he was quite attractive but what initially interested me was his crazy sense of humor. One night he had to come over on business and we talked. Toward the end of the evening he said,*
>
> *"What would you think of my moving in?"*
>
> *"Don't you think we should get to know each other first?" I asked. His answer was, "It's a good way to get to know each other." So we went to bed to check out the theory and he moved in the next day.*
>
> *The second night he was living here, he came home late and passed out at the kitchen table. It*

was my first indication he drank. After that, he came home stewed at least twice a week.

From the beginning, it was clear he didn't want to spend money on me. During the five months we lived together, we never went out together. He never took me to a restaurant. We ate at home. When I realized that I was buying most of the food, I mentioned, "Don't you think we should split the grocery expenses?" He earned about three times as much as me.

"Oh, no," he said, "I'll buy my own food." But he continued to eat mine. After a while I started to keep meat and frozen vegetables over at my sister's house.

The first month, he paid me half the rent. The second month I had to ask him for it and he started to hassle me. The schmucko said I had hang-ups about money. Even though he hadn't lived with his wife in several years, he'd never got an apartment of his own. Apparently he had lived with a succession of women, none of whom had requested contributions to their rents. "Wendall," I kept saying, "you wouldn't like me to keep you, would you?" That's exactly what he would have liked.

If I hadn't insisted that he leave, I'm convinced he'd be here right now.

The Corporate Pervert. Not only is the office rampant with married men, the woodwork of its paneled conference rooms is infested with perverts. In most cases, they are one and the same people.

An office pervert may or may not be The Boss. Without question, he will be the company president or the chairman of the board, also the 60-year-old messenger "boys" slobbering through their appointed rounds. Otherwise, the office pervert can be identified by his tedious stories about the missus and her brownie-baking marathons for the Blue

Birds, as well as the photographs of his kids (his wife is missing) which are prominently plasticubed on his desk.

Under the circumstances, a woman hesitates to offend by saying what she thinks. Instead, it's more politic to:

1. Act like a lady *(giggle)*.
2. Pretend she's his mother. "Really Henry, you're simply awful."
3. Change the subject. "I hear you've just been promoted to sales promotion manager."

A random selection from our files of office perverts reveals all of them to be solid family men:

THE PERVERT FROM THE PURCHASING DEPARTMENT - Jill struck up a conversation with a man while waiting in line at the Schrafft's wagon. A few weeks later he invited her out for a drink after work.

> *At the cocktail lounge he kept raving about a special seafood restaurant in Brooklyn, and finally he invited me to join him for dinner. He had a car and when we left the bar, he drove over to the river and down under the West Side Highway. He pulled into a parking lot near the docks and before I knew what was happening, he'd unzipped his fly, pulled out his thing, and asked me to give him a blow job.*
>
> *I kept saying, "I can't" and "What makes you think I'd do that?"*
>
> *During our conversation at the bar, he'd mentioned that he knew this TV celebrity, and I'd said, "How exciting. What's she like?" Well, get this, now he gets very angry and tells me, "___ did it to me." What an incredible line: I think he was psycho.*
>
> *I insisted he start the car and take me home. On the way, he informed me that I was a stupid bitch. I wanted to tell him that if he was so smart, he might have waited until after dinner before exposing himself.*

THE PERVERT FROM THE EXECUTIVE SUITE - Nora greatly admired the president of her company, a friendly fellow who made a point of asking for her professional opinions, even if it meant calling her at home. She was flattered by his attention. Prior to this incident, there had been a number of luncheons and evening phone calls.

> *He would call to talk about business, politics, theater. Everyday subjects like that. He was married and had five children. He talked a lot about the kids. I was curious about whether he called me from home. I wondered what his family thought. "Sure," he said once, "I'm calling from the den."*
>
> *One night his breath sounded funny. "What's wrong?" I asked. "You seem to be having trouble breathing." I thought maybe he had a cold.*
>
> *"Keep talking," he wheezed. "Don't stop. Keep talking." I felt sick.*
>
> *I asked him if his wife were home. She was in the living room watching television. I said good-bye and hung up. I thought, "You filthy pig."*
>
> *After that, I never liked to talk to him on the phone. I had this picture of him, sitting there jerking off a few feet away from his wife and kids. How sick can you get?*

THE PERVERT WHO'S YOUR BOSS - Betsy's supervisor took a fatherly interest in her personal life:

> *It's hard to separate a pervert who exposes himself on the street from a normal man. I think of men like Ron as little boys who grew up thinking sex is bad and when they unleash their fantasies on some poor girl, they unload a whole bag of shit.*
>
> *When I told him that I'd been mugged and robbed, he gave me a lecture on taking taxis and how I should be more careful. Well, everything he says pisses me off but I wasn't about to be nasty.*

> *"Yes, yes, you're right," I said. Then he asks, "Did they make any sexual advances?" I told him, "No. They just gave me a smack and knocked my glasses off." He says, "You could have been raped."*
>
> *He seemed to relish the thought because he practically was licking his lips. So I told him that if they'd tried, I would have kicked their balls in and he changed the subject.*
>
> *He's always asking, "How's your social life, ha, ha?" Meaning, how's my sex life, of course. Does he think I'm going to tell him; I just say, "Oh, I get around."*

THE OBSCENE CALLER IN THE BROOKS BROTHERS SUIT - Sara, who is self-employed, works from her home. Simon is one of her clients.

> *Simon doesn't imagine his fantasies. He talks them. For months he would call me at 9 a.m. and when anybody calls at that hour, I figure they want to talk about business.*
>
> *"How's your lovely cunt?" he'd say. He was at his office.*
>
> *"Simon," I'd answer, "I hope your door is closed." What I wanted to say was, "Eccchhh."*
>
> *He was so dense that he greeted any answer I made with guffaws of laughter. He was titillated that I had enough nerve to reply. If guys like him were ever confronted by the real thing, they wouldn't know what to do.*

Men may be right after all. The office is no place for a woman. However, as experiences go, it is not a complete waste of time. Little Darling has discovered the truth about Daddy, but, better yet, she now knows what to expect from the man she marries. As it says in the Miss Clairol ad, "Today's no-nonsense gal wants all the facts."

FOUR

I Guess You Could Say She's That Cosmopolitan Girl

I Guess You Could Say She's That Cosmopolitan Girl

Sex used to be the single woman's vintage game. If she could manage to preserve the sanctity of her genitals until precisely the right moment, she was able to set herself up comfy for life as a wife, and stop worrying about food and rent. A lot of other expenses, she hoped, would be taken care of as well. The only drawback, a minor one to be sure, was that sexual test-marketing was out of the question. Frequently she wound up with a pig in a poke and never knew the difference.

Since the so-called Sexual Revolution, the new climate of permissiveness encourages a woman to bounce from Simmons to Simmons without concern for morals. In fact, now that virginity is generally regarded as a terminal disease requiring immediate surgery, the woman disinclined to treat her crotch as a subway turnstile is worse than a prude. She's an infantile human being whose inability to relate makes her an ideal candidate for therapy.

Seeing as how the post-revolutionary era is hardly the promised land, bedroom politics remains more crucial than ever for single women. Their games will be familiar to anyone who has dipped into the writings of Helen Gurley Brown or the other experts who have given unmarried women such a bad name. Their strategies, so men claim, are both obvious and odious. But what men don't hear are the asides women say to each other as they execute the rusty old routines.

So will the *real Cosmo* "girl" please stand up and tell us all about the men in her life?

I. SEX OBJECT GAMES

The Education of a Sex Object. In one respect or another, men appear to be obsessed with their penises almost every minute of the day. Even nocturnally, if we are to believe them, they emit. Apparently they think that women should be equally preoccupied with their genitals. At least they hope so because the suspicion that women may not be devoting their entire attention to some part of their bodies can only mean at worst that they are using their brains and at best that they aren't spending every living moment thinking about men. Since the former is considered a subversive activity, many women feel it's best not to disillusion them.

What men don't seem to comprehend is that a sex object isn't made overnight. It takes seventy or eighty years of constant practice. Many people never succeed.

Nevertheless, women persevere because, if nothing else, it presents a challenge to their intellects. When permissible mental stimulation is limited, you take what you can get. That's why men create Mona Lisas while the Mona Lisas are busy shaving the hair from their legs and armpits. Where else could women find such a perfect ready-made activity to fill up so many hours of a lifetime?

For all that, the basic reason we become sex objects is that it's the sole means of capturing male attention. From the beginning, Little Darling recognized that looking pretty was the way to get attention and affection from Daddy. For the remainder of her nubile years, sex appeal will be her chief means of Getting—Getting a free meal, Getting a job, Getting a husband. Since recognition is impossible, attention will have to do.

Besides, refusal to look fetching immediately draws unfavorable attention to oneself. Unless a woman makes an attempt to appear sexy by displaying her equipment out in plain view, suspicions are aroused. Maybe, men decide, she's a dyke. Inasmuch as they aren't able to distinguish a lesbian from the Playmate of the Month, this is an hilarious conclusion. But a woman can't be too careful.

With the guidance of *Mademoiselle* and *Cosmo,* she selects some portion of her body which is "good," *i.e.,* valued by men, and then proceeds to showcase it. Breasts and bottom are the two most popular.

While a man may want to marry a girl just like the girl who married dear old Dad, and usually does exactly that, he isn't crazy about dating one who looks like her. Instead of Mother in her rump-sprung chenille, he'd rather have a girl with a firm C-cup and a tight-cheeked behind. This lets out most women over sixteen, but he doesn't notice. One self-styled connoisseur of female backsides is Irv, a thirtyish, baldish accountant disguised as a hippie. Jill met him at a party:

> *That night I was wearing tight jeans, no bra, and my contacts because if I go to a party looking everyday-normal, nothing happens. This stud sidles over to me and says his name is Irv. "I'm an ass man," he announces. I mean, how gross can you get? But I guess he meant it as a compliment. He must have assumed that anyone who exhibits their tushie in jeans couldn't have anything upstairs because he treated me as if I were slightly retarded.*
>
> *"Are you from Brooklyn?" he asked condescendingly. There's a whole connotation about women from Brooklyn; they're supposed to be dopey. Either they're secretaries or they're being supported by their parents.*
>
> *"Okay," I thought, and went along with the joke. It was giggle-giggle for the rest of the night. I went out with him once after that but then I couldn't take any more.*

Also wandering around are large numbers of people who expose themselves as "leg men." Sandy furnishes a laywoman's analysis of a leg man:

> *The guy will say, "You've got a nice pair of legs." Now, depending on my state of mind at the*

> *time, I try to feel flattered. However, since I don't think my legs are anything special, it's obvious he's handing me a line.*
>
> *The thing that makes me uptight about such comments is that I always feel he's out to fuck me. My legs have nothing to do with it.*

The well-bred lecher sticks to the safety of a time-tested routine, "You have such nice eyes." When Barbara hears his old-fashioned love song, she's doubly on guard. A serenade to an eye man:

> *"Oh really?" I say. "They're all right. I have two." I never consider such a ridiculous statement a compliment. This is the guy who you just know brags to his buddies the next day, "I really went home with a dog last night but what're ya gonna do? When ya wanna get laid and they're puttin' out, ya take what ya can get."*
>
> *When a man talks about your eyes, he always turns out to be some son of a bitch like that.*

Feminine and Masculine Hygiene. When the first vaginal spray deodorants were introduced a few years ago, Madison Avenue faced a truly tricky problem: what to call the place they go. One advertising agency came up with a euphemism for the vagina which has got to be wonderfully, coquettishly male: "That part of you that is most woman." Although possibly there were a few women who missed the point because they imagined their core elsewhere, the message was clear to most. It only proved what we always suspected. Men think female genitals stink. For example, when Barbara was twenty, she met a man in a bar one night:

> *He'd been sitting there all evening touching himself. Finally I said, "Why don't we go for a ride?"*
>
> *He jumped up, paid for the drinks, and ran me*

> *out the door. We were necking on the bed in this sleazy, East Side hotel when he pulled out two rubbers and started blowing up one of them. It broke. Nervous because he had only one left, he got started. Suddenly I heard him say, "Oh-oh." After he pulled out, I saw that the second rubber had broken, too. He didn't know what to do then. I refused to blow him so he said, "Okay, I'll go down on you and jack myself off." I wasn't enthusiastic because a man had never done that to me before but I thought, "Oh, what the heck."*
>
> *"Go wash yourself off," he told me. I washed and laid down again but as he was doing it to me, I kept wondering, "Why did he want me to wash? Does he think I'm dirty? Why is it all right to fuck me unwashed but he can't put his mouth on me?"*
>
> *I told him to stop and I started to put my clothes on.*
>
> *He sat there saying, "Whatsamatter? Whatsamatter?"*
>
> *"Nothing," I said. "Forget it and take me home."*

Always cooperative when it comes to buying new products, women spend over fifty million dollars a year to fumigate their genitals with benzethomium chloride, hexachlorophene, perfume, and God knows what other chemicals. Apparently we smell so vile that even soap and water is useless. Despite the propaganda, however, women have trouble believing their natural odor is all that offensive. Annabel, at sixteen, feels ambivalent:

> *I dunno. I kind of like the smell. I also know I'm not supposed to like it. I've decided it's a draw. Maybe I will reserve final decision until some man tells me whether I smell or taste good.*

On the other hand, there's the male organ, the lily-of-the-valley-sweet, germ-free, Saran-skinned penis. Generally we love it or leave it. Women may complain that it doesn't work but rarely do we publicly criticize the penis from the standpoint of hygiene. A sampler of random thoughts on male plumbing:

> 1. *"I find the smell of an aroused male rather sickening. Semen smells like ... I don't know what? The stench of it gets into your nostrils and clothes."*
> 2. *"I met this very eager guy at a party and took him home. He was so eager that he came before he got it in. I was sorry I'd ever invited him because my sofa never recovered. I had to buy a special cleaning fluid but if you look closely, the spots are still there."*
> 3. *"Semen stains. Like snot, it's virtually impossible to get off your clothes. I always say, 'Once you get snot on your raincoat, forget it.'"*
> 4. *"Men talk about the way women smell. They advise us to go out and buy cunt deodorants. By God, people who live in glass houses..."*

Penises We Have Known. Like the rest of his sex, Freud was a victim of The Penis Mystique. Not content to let it go at that, he went on to conclude that every woman must want one. He had to be kidding. Since it is men, not women, who suffer from penis envy, Freud seems to have viewed the problem backwards.

It's true, women do run into difficulties with the male parts, but not the ones Freud imagined. As genitals go, we find the penis grossly overrated. To tidy up the record a bit, here are some thoughtful observations from weenie-watchers:

> 1. "Absurd-looking."
> 2. "A limp dick isn't very cool."
> 3. "Only when I'm horny would I like to meet one."
> 4. "How did Sylvia Plath describe it? Turkey neck and turkey gizzard."

5. "Did you ever watch a guy make? It's hysterical. Why don't men wipe themselves? They just stand there and wait until it drip-dries."
6. "Once I was with a guy who insisted I feel him getting a hard-on. It was like touching a worm. Since I've never cared much for worms, I was totally turned off."

In Kathleen's family, the women refer to the male organ as "that thing":

> *Women may admire the penis when they're with men but among themselves, they laugh. That's the way it is in my family. I remember when my Uncle Lester wanted to sleep in the nude. My aunt claimed that she told him, "Don't you dare get into bed like that. I don't want to wake up in the morning and see that thing."*
>
> *Maybe she did say it but women only joke like that when men aren't around.*

Jokes aside, the penis is a problem serious enough to deserve closer political analysis. For a single woman, penis games require diplomacy, brinkwomanship, and split-second timing. The virgin, for example, plays Thank You for a Lovely Evening, a largely self-taught game which goes like this: After spending several hours with a man who supposedly wants nothing but the pleasure of her company, she's back at her front door or wherever she's selected in advance to cut him off. A few minutes later, a frontal assault is being aimed directly at her thigh. As soon as decently possible, she mentions the time—it's always late—and hastily finesses the game to a close with Thank You for ...

This game only requires a woman to act dumb and blind. If she choreographs the scene with sincerity, his feelings won't be hurt. He might conclude she's Catholic. Serving as an all-purpose technique which single women retain in their sexual repertory once they cease to be virgins, this simple rebuff can be used on practically any man a woman doesn't want. The slippery part is delivering the punch line before the situation turns awkward. Unfortunately, Thank You for ... must be abandoned at precisely that phase of her life when she'll feel most in need of it: When she becomes a wife.

Obviously, a woman who desires a confrontation is going to take a different approach to the penis. She wants satisfactory performance, something uncommonly hard to find these days. Sara, a woman of action and a compulsive basket cruiser, maintains that the size of a penis is important. Short of carrying a tape measure, there's no sure way to determine this in advance. But before she commits herself, she sizes up the situation as best she can. The secrets of a short-arm inspector:

> *If I suspect a guy isn't big, forget it. I hate a small one. On the beach, for instance, one way I check them out is by looking. Or if the man has an erection, I get a fairly good idea. It's more difficult when he's wearing a suit but if I like him well enough, I go by my vibes and hope for the best.*
>
> *Sometimes there are unpleasant surprises. Chemistry-wise, I was terribly attracted to Ben, the veterinarian, but he turned out to be small and thin. He couldn't satisfy me if he tried for a million years. But since I'd already undressed, I had to sleep with him once. I couldn't say, "No thanks, you're too teeny." But never again.*
>
> *The biggest one I ever saw is Patrick's. Long and fat. Unbelievable. The trouble is, he's a rotten human being.*

Since there seems to be a direct correlation between a man's self-esteem and his penis, it's easy to spot the fellow who worries about whether his is big enough. Usually he's agitated about several other things as well—his height, his mother, his waning creativity—all of which he dumps on any woman luckless enough to climb into bed with him. She can ignore his penis problem in the hope—that will be the day—it will go away by itself. Or she might boldly bring up the subject and trust her faith healing effects an overnight cure:

Faith Healer: That's some big schlong you've got there.
Peewee: Oh, do you think so?
Faith Healer: Yes, I've been admiring it. Gorgeous.

A scrawny penis should deserve no comment. Why create trouble? However, sooner or later the man with an anemic scallion forces his bed partner into playing critic-at-large whether she wants to or not:

Anemic: I hope it was okay.
Critic: It was wonderful.
Anemic: I was a little worried. I'm on the small side...
Critic: Uh, you look perfectly normal to me.
Anemic: I guess you've been with a lot of guys before?
Critic: Um, enough. It's not what you've got, it's what you do with it.
Anemic: Right.

Anemic's opposite number is the man who treats his genitals like the crown jewels. Nora remembers an episode with her ex-husband's penis in the days before they married:

After we began to sleep together, he left a pair of pajamas and toothbrush and razor at my apartment because he stayed on Saturday nights. His mother didn't like it but, after all, he was twenty-eight.

He also brought a can of Johnson's Baby Powder which I assumed he was going to use as an after-shave talcum. But after we'd have sex, I noticed he always dashed into the bathroom. One night I followed him. He was washing his penis, then he carefully dried it and sprinkled it with the baby

> *powder. He smoothed it around, just so, and then shook it off.*
>
> *I didn't know whether to laugh or to kill him. He made me feel dirty. I'd contaminated his precious baby cock. "Well," I finally said to myself, "he's just super-hygienic."*

The myth of the powerful penis is such an easily pricked legend that, to borrow from Dr. David Reuben, any woman can. And quite a lot do. They see that men have no control over their penises; they get erections at the most unseemly times and places. April refers to the mystique surrounding the male organ as the "tyranny of the penis."

> *Every fucking thing is supposed to be a phallic symbol. You have a dream about a pencil, it's a phallic symbol, right? It means you want to get laid, right? Well, goddamn it, wrong. A pencil is a pencil.*
>
> *As far as I can see, the "art" of having an erection is no different than a knee tapped with a hammer. The foot goes up.*

II. STREET GAMES

Ogling. Girl-watching, the all-male outdoors sport, is mankind's subtle way of reminding us that they own all the world, including the street. From the moment a woman steps foot out of her home alone, she knows that she's on enemy territory. Her only protection against lip-smacks, leers, and uncalled-for remarks is a male escort. Otherwise, out on the sidewalks it's open season any time of the year.

Admittedly, there's a foolproof antidote for ogling: A woman can stay home. But since she has to go out every now and then, this is a solution of questionable merit. Evenings, of course, are a different matter. Any woman who dillydallies on the street after dark is likely to be taken for, what else, a streetwalker. Golda Meir offers a suggestion worthy of further investigation:

> *Once, in the cabinet, we had to deal with the fact that there had been an outbreak of assaults on women at night. One minister suggested a curfew; women should stay home after dark. I said, "But it's the men who are attacking the women. If there's to be a curfew, let the men stay at home. Not the women."*

Oglers claim to be friendly fellows who have nothing more than irrepressible admiration for women; their gratuitous glances and remarks, they insist, are meant as flattery. Not unreasonably then, ogling invariably begins with a compliment:

> *Ogler: "Hey baby, I'd love to lick your pussy." (Or, "Wanna get fucked?" / "Lemme lick your cunt," / et cetera. Since oglers have limited vocabularies, their routine is never exactly full of surprises.)*
> *Flattered Woman: ("…..")*

Since there is no way to show her appreciation, a woman accepts the tribute in silence and removes herself from the scene as nimbly as possible. Attempts to outflank the ogler generally backfire:

> *Ogler: "Wanna get laid, honey?"*
> *Woman: "Fuck you."*
> *Ogler: "That's what I'd like to do."*

Counter-ogling ("Look at the basket on that one") tends to be unproductive because men scurry away, screaming for a crackdown on prostitutes. As a result, women mind their own business while unobtrusively observing men on the street. Generally, it's hard to find much worth looking at, but this is not always the case. Listen in on the oral graffiti of female oglers:

> 1. *"When I see guys adjusting their jock straps on the street or subway, I think, 'Come on, buddy, nobody's balls could be that big!'"*
> 2. *"There's the man who takes up two seats on the bus because he has to spread his legs. He thinks his peter is so big that he can't possibly close his thighs."*
> 3. *"The ones I love are the scratchers. They never seem to itch anywhere but between their legs. Like they suffered from diaper rash."*
> 4. *"When the weather gets hot, men's balls hang an inch lower."*
> 5. *"I've noticed most men wear their penises by their left legs; the left ball is usually lower than the right."*
> 6. *"A salesman, for example, will be standing there talking to you and then you notice his hands in his pockets, fondling his pee-pee. Men are constantly touching themselves."*

The men who get most of the credit for ogling are construction workers, truck drivers, and sanitation collectors, a clear example of class prejudice. In reality, the ogler just as often turns out to be somebody's Daddy. One morning Felicia was addressed by an executive ogler, presumably on his way to work:

> *I was pushing Melanie in her stroller when I heard someone call, "Oh baby ..." For a second I thought he was talking to the child and then the rest sunk in "... how'd you like a hot cock up your ass?"*
>
> *Out of the corner of my eye I saw he was a nicely-dressed business type in his forties, carrying a paper and an attache case. "My God," I thought, "if his wife could hear him now."*

Pickups. Since a woman encounters far more available men in public places than she does through formal introductions, she might as well take advantage. Eliminating the obscene ogler whose grandiose promises probably mean he's impotent, she allows herself to be picked up by a chicken ogler, preferably one hanging around a respectable establishment like a library, museum, or art gallery.

> *Chicken Ogler: "Remarkable how the Bauhaus influenced architecture and design after the Second World War." ("Hey baby, I'd love to lick your pussy.")*
> *Pickup: "Yes, that's occurred to me when I look at a Kandinsky." ("I wonder if he'd take me to Shirley's party on Saturday?")*

If all goes well, she should be able to cadge an invitation for a drink or dinner on the spot and, eventually, keep him as a regular date. However, a certain percentage of failure is to be expected. While waiting to cash a check at Bankers Trust Company, Sandy attracted the attention of a young, sharply-dressed, pipe-smoking ogler:

> *When I left the bank, he followed me. At the corner he spoke: "Would you like to join me for a drink?"*
>
> *"Oh sure," I said. I figured the worst he could be was married. At the bar, the first thing he wanted to know was if I were a lesbian. "My God," I said to myself, "is something showing?" Whatever it was, I was dying to find out so that I could cover it up. He said he could fix me up with a really beautiful woman and then he proceeded to relate, in detail, incredibly raunchy stories about how he had arranged orgies for a couple of movie stars.*
>
> *As it turned out, he was not only married but a pimp and a dope pusher.*
>
> *Finally the conversation got around to his fucking me. My place was out because of my roommate. When I suggested renting a hotel room,*

> *he suddenly remembered an appointment. I was so disappointed that I spilled my drink.*
>
> *The last I saw of him, he put me in a cab and slipped me some money for the fare. Little did he dream that his stories supplied me with fantasies for many joyful hours of masturbating.*

It's enough to destroy a woman's faith in human nature.

III. SEX GAMES

The Market Value of Virginity. In olden days, vaginas commanded respect. Despite scoundrels who tried to divide women into "nice girls" and "girls who put out," the shrewd woman wasn't fooled. Though she was forced to deny her sexuality, the stakes stood too high to risk tossing away a lifetime meal ticket. Eating has always meant more to us than screwing, although most of us still have to do one to get the other.

If reminded often enough, a decent man could be counted on to observe the ground rules of Virginity:

> *Decent Man: "Please."*
> *Virgin: "No."*
> *Decent Man: "But I love you."*
> *Virgin: "Not until we're married."*

Irrespective of the filthy things said about Virginity, it worked.

Knowing that she possessed one commodity men prized, a woman used her vagina as her chief negotiating tool and made damn certain to withhold it until she'd completed the sale. Beginning at puberty, she hung a dollar sign on her crotch and grew to womanhood with the comforting expectation of becoming either a wife or a prostitute. That so many have rejected the second profession is no doubt due to its reputation for being an unpleasant lifestyle. Obviously an information gap exists because, at least when prostitution flourished in the grand style, it offered a far more sensible life than marriage. By recycling her vagina, a woman was able to earn income from it over and over. At the same time, she was under no obligation to provide banal services like starched shirts and hot meals.

The disadvantage, let's say it, is old age. No man wants to pay for sex with an old whore. Of course he doesn't want to pay for it by supporting an old wife either, but he's legally obligated. That, thank heavens, was what made Virginity worthwhile in the long run.

If there was one thing both prostitutes and prospective wives recognized as bad business, it was the error of distributing free samples. Now that vaginas have fallen on hard times, and men expect us to give them away, their market value has plunged to zero. We take what we can get:

1. A cheeseburger with a side order of french fries.
2. A joint.
3. A "meaningful relationship," *i.e.*, sex without security.

Should today's woman reach the age of twenty-one with her withering hymen still intact, she feels compelled to attend to the problem. If she has the money, she visits a therapist who will suggest she doesn't like men. After several years of analysis, she will be able to cite ten specific reasons *why* she doesn't like men, any one of which prevents her from getting into bed with them. But finally, pulling herself together, she makes up her mind to get it over with. Professional de-flowerers being in short supply, Mary Beth reached the age of twenty-five before she resolved her crisis with a bartender:

> *I decided it was time. Frankie wasn't exactly good-looking but I picked him because he was there. I didn't tell him I was a virgin. Why should I? Anyway, it wouldn't have made any difference*

> *to him. An uncovered manhole would have suited him just as nicely.*
>
> *For five years my diaphragm had been lying around gathering cobwebs and now I had my big chance to use it. But he wouldn't hear of going to my apartment. "Oh no," he said, "My apartment is closer and we can tuck it right in." He used no contraceptive nor did I ask him to. In my relations with men, I'm usually extremely submissive. I don't say much.*
>
> *Afterwards he fell asleep and when I woke in the morning he was gone. I noticed the sheets were a bloody mess so I neatly pulled up the covers and thought, "Oh Frankie, are you in for a surprise." Then I went home and started counting. I never saw him again.*
>
> *I've since discovered that lots of times it's better to hop into bed with a strange man. Because once you do get to know him, you wouldn't want to.*

Mother was lucky. Expecting defloration to be dismal, she gritted her teeth and prayed it would be over quickly. The liberated virgin is supposed to enjoy it, when, in truth, she may feel just like Mother. At eighteen, Nora fell in love with a law student. The only detail to spoil her romance were Alexander's erections:

> *For over a year I managed to hold him off, first because I was living at home and then I went away to college. One weekend when I snuck away from school and flew to Michigan to visit him, we went to his grandmother's house for Sunday dinner. Pretty soon she put on her hat and gloves and announced she was going to church while the chicken cooked. The minute she was out the door, he said we had an hour. It was now or never.*
>
> *The only excuse I could think of was to say I'd get pregnant. "Don't worry," he told me. "I'll use*

rhythm." I had no idea what he meant, and still don't, because he didn't use anything.

It felt like an operation. Afterward I was numb. When his grandmother came home, we all sat down at the table as if nothing had happened.

Three weeks later I realized I was pregnant.

When Sara graduated from high school, she wanted to become an actress. Impatient for life, she didn't mind parting with her virginity even when her initiator happened to be a paunchy, thirty-eight-year-old whose name now escapes her:

> *Daddy paid for my defloration. It cost him $300 to send me to apprentice at the summer stock theater.*
>
> *I'd barely unpacked when I developed mad crushes on both the director and the leading man. When the director asked me to come to his room one night, I was thrilled. I snuck in and, half an hour later, snuck out. He told me to keep it a secret. Later I found out that he'd deflowered half the girl apprentices on the East Coast. But that summer I was crazy about him.*
>
> *The following week the leading man tried to make me. Since I couldn't do it with both of them and I certainly didn't want to hurt anyone's feelings, I told him I was a virgin. He didn't insist; instead, he suggested that I go down on him.*
>
> *I obliged. What did I know?*

O Seduction. When God created humans, She made one hell of a big mistake by inventing only two sexes. By now it's clear that women need more choices. Unfortunately, most of us are stuck with men.

A few sensible women have concluded that since females are nicer to begin with, why not sleep with our own kind. As tempting as this philosophy may sound, the average woman already has enough troubles to contend with. As Mary Beth sums up the dilemma:

> *I really would like to try it with a woman but I'm chicken.*

The alternative is to take a man to bed. Despite the "revolution," sex of a woman's own choosing is by no means easily accessible. For a male, sex is usually lying around if he looks hard enough. If one woman isn't willing, another is. But even the most aggressive woman has trouble openly approaching a partner she desires. Saddled with the notion that she should wait to be asked, she selects either from what drifts up to her doorstep or she plays games. O Seduction works most successfully when a woman says as little as possible.

PROLOGUE - Shave legs and underarms. Depilate mustache. Tweeze eyebrows. Bathe. Deodorize armpits and vagina. Wash, set, tease, comb hair (or spend eight dollars on a wig set). Lacquer nails. Find clean underwear, preferably lacy. Select clothing to reveal one or all of the following: breasts, rear, hips, legs. Glue on eyelashes. Paint face. Spray perfume. Limber up with a few last-minute shuffles.

After this considerable investment of time and money, she's ready for action. Unfortunately, the type of person attracted by her getup is not always what she has in mind because gamy street corner bums are just as likely to pick up her message. Indeed, by the time she arrives at her destination, she's already been inspected and screwed by a battalion of fantasizing passers-by, all of them male.

THE MAIN EVENT - Zeroing in on a likely candidate, she hustles into her routine. Meaning that she:

1. Never states outright she wants to sleep with him.
2. Listens to him talk about *his* problems, *his* mother, *his* allergies.

3. Reveals only enough about herself to prove she's alive and breathing.
4. Displays varying degrees of awe and admiration.
5. Smiles.

THE FINALE - Chances are, nine times out of ten, that O Seduction will end in a Pyrrhic victory. Betsy seduces a Right Guard man:

> *We were lying on the floor in his living room when he suggested we move into the bedroom. After I'd undressed, I got into bed and waited. In the meantime, he's doing a whole big number: mumbling about his five o'clock shadow, buzzing around with an electric razor, spraying his underarms with Right Guard, pulling down the shades.*
>
> *Finally he gets down to business and three seconds later, it's over. Wham Bam Thank-You-Ma'am. The second time was a bit better but I knew right away he'd never be much good in bed.*
>
> *He was thirty-five and never married. A mama's boy, a real prince. And impotent, or just as good as.*

Masturbation. When a woman masturbates, she's guaranteed to be in bed with a person she likes. The other reason for masturbation is enjoyment.

Nothing drives her to it faster than marriage. Although Felicia has been married nine years, she didn't discover masturbation until recently, to her regret. A before and after testimonial:

> *I'd heard about orgasms. Until two years ago I'd never had one.*
>
> *Then I started to masturbate and I've been having orgasms ever since. My only guilt is that I haven't told Morris. He'd feel awful.*

While a wife must masturbate during office hours, the single woman can choose her time. But she, too, must be a closet masturbator. Jill questions the wisdom of telling a man about one's masturbatory pleasures:

> *At times I'm lying in bed afterwards and I can hardly wait to get dressed and go home. I'd love to say, "Pardon me, Nickie, but I have to run home to masturbate." God knows when he'd be able to get it up again.*

The trouble with masturbation is that for many years, maybe forever, a woman feels sure she's the only one who does it. It was the one sight which threw mother into cardiac arrest; even an enlightened mother didn't appreciate it. Boys, of course, were allowed to touch themselves, although it's hard to understand why they couldn't learn to sis-sis sitting down like everybody else. It's got to be more comfortable.

Despite early genital-washing, it's never too late to discover what your body is all about by means of creative masturbation. Chances are the circumstances will never be ideal for, while no longer under mother's eagle eye, a woman still can't be open. Men don't approve either; they tend to take it personally. Nora first investigated masturbation after a date with Charlie:

> *First he couldn't jack it up and then, whammo. Flash Gordon. He was one of those men always blowing off about their big deals, yapping about important appointments. Well, as soon as he'd finished, he grabs his cigar and away he goes. That was the first time I'd had the urge to masturbate. I remember giggling later because I thought, "Who needs men?" I could do a better job than most men I knew. I've always wanted to thank Charlie.*

Angela's introduction to the subject was unintentionally provided by a pornography buff, Conrad:

Every couple of months he used to get together with his buddies for a stag movie party. Whenever I asked if I could attend, he got very huffy. "The guys wouldn't like that," he said.

Then once when the party was at his place, I dropped by after everyone had gone home. Only one film interested me because it showed a woman masturbating. It looked like fun.

I guess Conrad showed me the movies to turn me on. They did. But not to him.

Gothic Abortion Tales. The single woman plays Abortion on two fronts at once.

1. With the man who impregnated her and,
2. With the abortionist, also a man and frequently a bigger prick than the impregnator.

In Round One of Abortion the woman serves notice that the sky has fallen. Informing the man at all is futile, of course, because nothing terrible has happened to him. Nevertheless, there are several reasons why she'll probably tell him, if she can find him:

1. Regardless of the circumstances, she figures he's to blame.
2. Her mother wouldn't understand.
3. Maybe the man can find her an abortionist.
4. She needs cash.

The last is crucial because rarely does a single woman have $500 or $1000 lying around loose. Neither may the man, but that's his headache.

The goal in Round Two is obtaining money, doctor, and possibly a modest amount of moral support. To maintain an amicable relationship with the man means ignoring the fact that he's more frightened than she and disguising her contempt because what's he got to be scared about? It also means ignoring his insinuations that he couldn't be responsible (The Somebody Else's Child Syndrome). Ditto for his whines that it's not easy to find an abortionist—or $500.

Round Three reruns two old favorite games, Smiling and Tears, until the moment when all arrangements are made. Such melodrama diverts the man's attention from knowing what is really on her mind. Murder. Not of the fetus which she cannot conceive of as a living thing. It's the man she wants to kill, but manslaughter being even less socially acceptable than abortion, she reminds herself to remain cordial. Any port in a storm.

After it's over, she's free to tell him what she thinks. If her experience has been uneventful (which is unlikely) she may decide to forgive (she never forgets) and assume an it-can-happen-to-anyone attitude which allows her to go on seeing the man. Or she can supply a blow-by-blow account in the hopes of torturing him.

In either case, she can't get around the fact that the man has been merely a spectator. There is no way to completely articulate the experience nor does she reveal her homicidal fantasies. A treasury of yarns about the silent partners in Abortion:

> 1. *"I hadn't seen or thought about Bill for five years and then I had this dream. I was running for a train, lugging a big, heavy suitcase. I was afraid the train would leave without me. Finally I got on, found a seat, unlocked the suitcase. I saw Bill's head in it. Just his head. So I closed the case and began to read* Time *magazine."*
>
> 2. *"Afterward he took me back to the hotel in a taxi and called room service to order champagne and lobsters. 'Wow, a party,' I said to myself. I was enraged that he should consider an abortion the occasion for a celebration."*
>
> 3. *"Our relationship continued for two years after*

the abortion. I kept telling myself that I was a big girl, responsible for my own actions. It wasn't his fault I got pregnant. I mean, nobody was really to blame. And yet I never felt the same about him after it. I think my love was tinged with loathing."

Meanwhile, there's the abortionist, a breed whose villainous reputation is richly deserved. In recent years abortionists have launched a magnificent public relations campaign to show what humanitarians they've been all along. Women know better. Step right up and meet our friend, the abortionist:

NORA'S FRIEND - The first thing he did was count my money. When I got on the table he said he couldn't use an anesthetic—he didn't explain why—and if it hurt, I should be careful not to make any noise. His office was on the second floor above a lot of stores and I could hear traffic and people talking. The bastard was right about it hurting. The pain was unbelievable. When I started screaming, he told the nurse to stuff a towel in my mouth. All during the operation, he talked: "You're getting just what you deserve." "Remember this next time you fuck." "If you think this is bad, wait until you have a baby."

I took the streetcar home and lay on my bed for the rest of the day. It was July, a very hot July, and I just lay there. I felt relieved, free, and full of hatred. The bastards have you coming and going. If they don't screw you one way, they find another.

For over ten years I couldn't even contemplate the idea of pregnancy without panicking.

ANGELA'S FRIEND - When he came into the room, he locked the door. Even before he unzipped his fly, I knew what was going to happen. As soon as he closed the door, I could see the whole picture.

> *He told me to spread my legs and put my feet in the stirrups. He knew and I knew that I wasn't going to say a word. Because my choice was to let him or walk out without the abortion. At that point I just didn't care.*
>
> *I don't remember a thing except that I felt dead. He could have been doing it to a dead body.*
>
> *As I was leaving, he said, "You're a very pretty girl, you know that?"*
>
> *Pig.*

Rape Me. Men continue to cherish the myth that women enjoy rape. Don't they read it in *Playboy*? What about the dreams and fantasies women whisper to the shrinks whose posh suburban hideaways they so good-naturedly support? However, the real reason men refuse to believe women don't like rape is that it conflicts with their personal experiences. The women *they* raped never complained.

Most women are raped by men they know: boyfriends, bosses, dinner companions, analysts, husbands, husbands' friends, friends' husbands, next-door neighbors. Or, as in Tanya's case, Mother may introduce her to a friendly rapist:

> *My mother fixed me up a date with a doctor she knew, a resident at ____ Hospital. When I arrived at the hospital to meet him, he took me on a tour of the ob-gyn ward where he worked. Then he suggested we go up to the residents' quarters for a drink. He put on some music and zappo, the next thing I knew he was unzipping his fly and pulling off my underpants. It happened so fast I don't know how he had time to get a hard-on. It was like he couldn't fuck his female patients so he decided to fuck the first healthy woman he came across that day. It happened to be me. I had met him before with my mother; he knew me. Why did he believe I would dig being raped?*

> *He was a huge man. about 260 pounds. I started screaming completely irrational things: "If you don't get off me. I'll walk out of here." When he was through, he went to the bathroom to wash up and shave. Then, as if nothing extraordinary had happened, he says, "I guess I got carried away. Let's go and eat." I couldn't think of a way to say no.*
>
> *We went to a luncheonette where I sat through the meal terrified. I kept thinking, "It must be my fault. This doctor wouldn't do anything really wrong. I must have led him on."*
>
> *And the whole time I'm worrying about how to get away, over to the West Side where my car was parked.*
>
> *Later I told a psychiatrist about the incident. He said it was my fault: I wasn't the victim but the perpetrator of the rape. That's why I went out to dinner afterward. That was all the confirmation I needed. I nearly killed myself with an overdose of sleeping pills.*
>
> *I have yet to tell my mother about this.*

But as a rule, women accept home-grown rape in the spirit intended, as a more or less benevolent gesture. Those with an excessively philosophical streak may even conclude that a mild rape now and then can't hurt.

Rape comes in a variety of disguises; the most common is when a woman goes to bed against her will because she hasn't felt free to say, "Up yours." When she gets laid in spite of herself, the rapist is usually a gentleman. Too well-bred to crouch in alleys, too timid to attack strangers who may be carrying a pocket-size can of Mace, the gentleman rapist seeks women who will love him. At twenty-six, Janet's aspirations were refreshingly traditional. She was in transit—to marriage, babies, a house with grass. When she met Arnold on Fire Island one summer, she spoke of love and marriage; Arnold spoke of love and a relationship. She said let's wait with the sex for a while; Arnold said she was prudish, sick, and selfish. And so:

> *I did it the weekend after Labor Day. It was awful. We were in bed at his apartment and I began to cry. I loved him but I felt such rage at being forced into sex before I wanted it. I hated his unspoken ultimatum: Lay me or I'll leave you.*

He left her anyway, for a Lufthansa stewardess.

A compendium of remarks on rape and rapists, gentlemanly and otherwise:

> Barbara
>
> *Men say we deserve to be raped because we wear low-cut dresses. Well, women should be able to walk on the streets without any clothes, the same way a man could. If a man were to go naked with his balls hanging out, I'm sure he could walk down any street in this country and never be raped by a woman. By other men, yes.*

> Kathleen
>
> *As a girl, I heard at retreats all the time, "You are the guardians of purity. Morality lies with Catholic womanhood. Remember, he is not responsible."*
>
> *The Church told us that sex is an animal thing but once we get married, it becomes our duty. Maybe that's why so many Catholic wives down deep believe their husbands are animals.*
>
> *Men are supposed to be logical, unemotional, and always thoroughly in control of the situation. And yet they can't control their passions. "Oh, tch, tch, look at that—he ripped that girl open like a chicken but he couldn't help it."*

> April
>
> *They get it on; we're supposed to get it off. It's our*

problem, not theirs. They don't take responsibility for anything. If they get into trouble, they bleat that a woman led them on. If they can't get it up, it's their mothers' fault. One way or another, they always hang it on a woman.

And a brusque encore from Jill

Men are slaves to their pricks.

What's a Nice Girl Like Me...? No doubt many women, including droves of wives, purchased *The Sensuous Woman* in hopes of getting a few tips to straighten out their crummy sex lives. Anyone who bought the book looking for serious instruction was bound to be disappointed. However, "J"'s how-to compilation for the paraprofessional prossie supplies a bounty of belly laughs because:

1. Few women would go the trouble of whipping fresh cream, adding a dash of vanilla and powdered sugar, spreading it on a dick, and then lapping it up. For $75, maybe; for free, no. In most cases she wouldn't even whip fresh cream for strawberry shortcake.
2. She wonders what the hell Penis/Mouth Techniques like The Butterfly Flick and The Hoover do for *her*.

Little Darling might wish she were a sensuous woman, but, at heart, she's content to be a puritan. However, since sexual kinkiness seems to be modish these days, she can count on meeting some scuzzbunny who insists they try out everything he's read. If she likes him, she swallows it. If she's like April, she spits it out:

When I was eighteen, I did it once because I felt compelled to. He told me I'd excited him, so it was my responsibility to take care of him. "Jerk off," I told him but he said that was for kids. As a man, he was entitled, right? I couldn't argue with that. So I blew him.

I thought I was going to suffocate. It felt like someone was jamming an ear of corn in my mouth. Because I didn't know anything about timing, I didn't stop him before he ejaculated in my mouth. I couldn't taste anything because I was too busy trying to breathe. But it was gagging, and I remember wanting to throw up.

"Give me a tissue," I said, "or I'll spit this all over you." I leaned out of the car window and made a big production of spitting. Pah, pah.

I felt vicious.

When Betsy was twenty-three and living at home, she met a medical student at her cousin's wedding. Believing, as she did at the time, that marrying a doctor was the epitome of success, she developed an instant affinity for Bernard. But in the end, Betsy regrets to report, he turned out to be literally a pain in the ass:

Later that summer he visited Cleveland again. Daddy felt sorry for him because he was a poor medical student and he wouldn't hear of Bernard staying at a hotel. "Don't spend money, my boy. You can't afford it." Daddy gave him the keys to our cottage at the lake.

We spent two days screwing. Never went out all weekend. On Sunday we were still in bed when he asked me if I knew about sodomy. "It's just another way to do it," he explained. Right then I had a sickening feeling that my beautiful picture of him was about to be shattered. His description definitely did not turn me on but he was doing such a good selling job, I thought, "Maybe I should give it a try at least." It was a disaster. Terribly painful. Worse than an enema. Bernard suggested Vaseline

> *might help. Finally I couldn't help yelling, "STOP! OUT!"*
>
> *And I'd really liked the odious bastard, too.*

IV. DATING GAMES

The Man Problem. Your average woman, including your average *Cosmo* "girl," wants to get married. In the interim, however, there's no reason why her expeditions in search of a husband shouldn't allow her to enjoy herself once in a while. One of the biggest unmentionables about dating is she gets out of the house at someone else's expense. The hitch is that she needs a man to do it. No woman would be crazy enough to pay for someone else's dinner and movie. A clue to the Man Problem is supplied by Mary Beth's recollection of a date with Al:

> *Part of the problem with dating is that I don't go out often enough. As a result, each man becomes enormously important. Take Al, this guy my sister fixed me up with. I'd never met him before. When he comes to pick me up, he makes himself at home on my couch, takes off his shirt, and says, "Massage my back." I was stunned. And even though I'm in Women's Lib, I found myself massaging his back.*
>
> *When you only go out once in a while, something terrible like that usually happens.*

Unless she dates, a single woman has no social life worth mentioning, none that's respectable, anyway. Two women entering a discotheque together would be immediately seated in the lesbian section; a lone woman with the prostitutes. Faced with this chilling prospect, a woman has no choice but dating men and damn if that doesn't mean sprucing up the puerile acrobatics she first learned in high school. She giggles, holds hands, snuggles, simpers, but mainly it's that legendary routine, Listening.

> *Date: "I, I, I, I, I, I, I, I, I, I."*
> *Woman: "How exciting! And then what did your boss say?"* I *"How awful! And then what did your mother say?"*

Speaking of men's mothers, a single woman has her sex life to consider. Linda brings up an unforgettable dentist named Herb:

> *At 4 one morning the phone rings in my apartment. "Quick," says Herbie. "Answer it. It might be my mother."*

Theoretically, dating could be a divine activity since it offers an unbeatable combination of freeloading, sex, and a chance to comparison shop for a husband. In reality, there are problems. Meet six of them:

> *DAVID (BETSY'S PROBLEM) - The first time I went out with him, I was determined to pull The Shirley Bit. My friend Shirley's philosophy is: Don't Do It on the First Date Just in Case You Decide to Marry Him.*
>
> *But for all my good intentions, I slept with him anyway. He was so pretty. Sex was beautiful. And it continued to be lovely every Saturday night for six weeks until one Saturday he lost his erection. Instead of relaxing, he got very nervous and started on a history of his sex life. About the girl who kicked him out and the girl who said devastating things about his virility. He had one story after another about the rotten way girls had treated him.*
>
> *Because naturally I felt guilty, I kept saying, "Well, you know, girls aren't really that bad." In the meantime, I was feeling so awful that I offered to help him get his erection back but he pushed my hand away. It was as if he were telling me, "Hands off, it's my property."*

While trying to get himself hard again, he continued with his sex history and took it back to the age of eleven when he'd apparently had a terrible time in the Bronx because people called him "that faggy little boy." Pretty soon, he got to his mother and the atrocities she had committed toward him.

I felt bad about him hating his mother but was it my fault? That's when I decided he wasn't for me. When I like a guy, I try to ignore signs that he may be screwed up. In the end, though, I'm repulsed.

When I broke our next date, I didn't tell him the truth. I couldn't hurt him.

HARVEY (MARIA'S PROBLEM) - On the beach in broad daylight, he talked dirty. With a crowd around, it was "motherfucker this" and "cunt that" and "let's fuck, baby." One of his standard lines was, "I'd like to eat you." I went along with the jokes and when I'd see him, I'd say, "Want to eat me today?"

Then we went to bed. I reminded him about eating. "A nice girl like you doesn't want that, do you?" Since I got the cue, I had enough sense to say, "Of course not."

He could barely hold on to his erection until he'd got it in. Although the whole thing lasted about forty seconds, I pretended not to notice. "Wow, great." I made so much noise I should have been a sound effects record.

Afterward he lay there snuffling and snorting, like he was really exhausted. I heard him mumble, "I think I love you." He thought! *I was so furious I wanted to cry but I just turned away and lay on the opposite edge of the bed. "I think I'll take a shower," he said, and on his way to the bathroom I heard him ask, "How about making me a tuna fish sandwich?"*

SANDOR (SANDY'S PROBLEM) - One night I went to ___'s with my sister. During dinner, the maitre d', a Hungarian, kept fawning over me. I had mixed feelings because if he'd been the owner of ___'s, it would have been better.

Anyway, I gave him my number and a few days later he called to ask me out to lunch. When he came for me, he brought flowers. This really impressed me because I'd grown up with all these romantic dreams of walking hand in hand through the park and love being a many-splendored thing. But, so far, all the men I'd met were these deadheads. At lunch everything was just the way I'd dreamed. He paid me lovely compliments in a thick, romantic Hungarian accent but something bothered me: I didn't believe one word he was saying. For crissakes, he didn't even know me.

When he brought me home, he pushed me up against the wall and kept muttering how lovely I was. It made me angry because, in my experience, attacks like that always happened at night. I couldn't tell if he had a hard-on or not, nor was I interested in finding out. He went away annoyed but the next morning, a dozen red roses arrived. That did it. I was positive he was a phony. I would never go out with him again.

My sister kept asking, "Whatever happened to Sandor? He was such a nice guy." I'd say, "I don't like him. He's oily."

BARRY (SARA'S PROBLEM) - Barry was a podiatrist. He schlepped around with his Playboys *and* Penthouses *because, like most thirty-year-old men, he couldn't do much else.*

By the time he got it up, he was pooped. Then he'd fuck very fast, like he was pumping air into a tire. He'd huff and puff and pump away and then he'd say, "Wow, I've been going five minutes. How do you like THAT?" Huff, puff.

Particularly in the mornings, he had to hurry or he'd lose his erection. Because if we'd done it the night before, it was too much to ask that he repeat the performance.

Barry was pencil-thin, even with a hard-on. Sex was bad enough with such a skinny penis but then his dog would try to jump in bed with us. The dog had a bigger penis than he did.

CLARENCE (KATHLEEN'S PROBLEM) - He was an insane writer who lived in a brownstone on the West Side. His room was filled with suitcases full of notebooks and manuscripts. I liked him a lot except he had this hang-up: He was impotent. Until I realized that fact, I thought it was my fault, even though he was always blaming it on something like alcohol or the lateness of the hour.

Now that I look back, Clarence was pretty hysterical. He liked to tell me about the wet dreams he'd had the night before. I think he must have suffered from premature ejaculation. Premature by twenty-four hours.

DANIEL (BONNIE'S PROBLEM) - I met him at a singles party. He was thirty-eight, a Ph.D. in economics, never married. He made a nice salary. At first, I was enthusiastic because obviously he was very intelligent.

But after the first few dates, it was apparent he couldn't relate to people. Finally I said, "You don't know much about me, do you?" So on the next date, right after sex, we were in bed and he asked me ten questions by rote: my background, who had proposed to me, what year, why hadn't I married him? His immaturity showed in his handwriting which was as atrocious as a ten-year-old's.

> *Slowly he bored me to death. I remember one night we saw* A Man for All Seasons *and then went to the Russian Tea Room to talk. I mean,* he *talked. The whole evening he lectured me as though we were in a classroom. I had an abcessed tooth that week. I was in agony.*
>
> *Orgasms come easily for me but I didn't have them with him. But I made believe I was having a good time and figured, "Well, maybe next time it will be different." And I didn't like doing that at all.*
>
> *He finished so fast that I hardly knew he was inside me. Once he asked, "Was I too fast?" I wanted to say, "Is it over?" but I think I answered, "Yeah." Just "Yeah." I should have said "fuck you" and masturbated.*
>
> *Later I tried to show him how to satisfy me but as soon as he'd do something that worked, he'd stop and go back to his old way. It sounds absurd but he didn't know where a woman's pleasure points are located. I'm surprised he could find my vagina.*
>
> *When I told him on the phone that I couldn't go out with him any more, he made some dig about my sexual hang-ups.*

The Playgirl Philosophers.

No man wants to be treated like an object. After all, he's an individual, a sensitive human being full of traumatic feelings about his mother. Except for a few ball-busters (dykes most likely), he has never known a real woman who didn't go out of her way to appreciate his uniqueness.

Him a sex object? Preposterous. To begin with, he knows that gals aren't fussy about men in bed. It's not their nature.

> *(Sara: "To be satisfied, it's not necessary for me to have an orgasm every time. But if I don't have one*

> *almost every time, you can be damn sure I'm going to dump the guy.")*

These days gals may yap a lot about orgasms but he needn't concern himself on that score. The chicks he takes to bed always have orgasms.

> *(Maria: "I don't really fake them, it's more a case of not saying anything because nobody asks me. Men don't even know when you've had an orgasm.")*

Besides, if there's a subject he's really up on, it's female sexuality.

> *(Bonnie: "Men are very Victorian. They aren't at all aware of women's sexuality. Most of them get their ideas from reading* Playboy. *They believe a woman should lie* under them, *mind you, with her legs spread.")*

He's read in the Times *that a growing number of men are complaining about impotence. A shame but, thank God, he won't have to worry about that problem for another twenty years.*

> *(Maria: "Most men I know are more or less impotent. Certainly the generation over thirty has to see porno movies because they're sexually wiped out.")*

But, knock on wood, even should he slow down some day, there will always be some chick happy to sleep with him. A tired penis is better than no penis, har, har.

> *(Sara: "If I should decide to give up on men completely, I'd buy a vibrator. I could have a perfect sex life because I'd have great sex when I wanted it. I would be masturbator of my own fate, har, har.")*

All a gal really wants is one guy to love and admire. She doesn't really dig casual sleeping around the way a man does.

> *(Maria: "I've had my most fantastic orgasms on one-night stands. It's always beautiful the first time because there's the kissing and the buildup to sex. After that, it inevitably goes down hill. Men stop kissing.")*

When it comes right down to it, gals just don't enjoy sex as much as guys.

> *(Maria: "Men talk about sex but they don't enjoy it as much as we do. I get horny when I douche. Girls don't have to wait to get it up; I could do it five times in a row without getting tired.")*

For all their experience, even the most liberated gals today don't know their way around in the sack. As long as you show them a good time, dinner, a movie maybe, they're satisfied without you acting like a stud.

> *(Sara: "Superstud was a snobby account executive I met in a bar on 45th Street. Not only did he turn out to be terrific in bed, but he also looked like Glen Campbell. I had been suffering a long dry spell then and, for once, I got enough.")*

> *(Maria: "Sy could keep it up for an hour at a time, sometimes two. It would go down and come right back up again. Only went soft once in the two years I dated him. Dynamite!")*

Take it from him, man, sexual performance isn't the most important thing. What gals really want is a full relationship with a guy. Communication. Open exchange of feelings.

(Bonnie: "After the first time, the courting was over. After a month, there was no necking. Once he'd succeeded in getting me to bed, he figured he could shortcut from Step One to Step Ten. All he cared about was getting his nuts off. Oh, I suppose I could have worked at making sex better but it was too big a job. The situation called for a therapist to get in bed with us and guide him by the hand. Actually, there were so many other things I didn't like about him; sex was just part of it.")

So there you are.

The Goldilocks Papers - *That summer I was feeling like Miss America. Finally I had accepted the fact that I would never grow any taller than five-foot-two. I had lost a lot of weight so I looked pretty good.*

One afternoon in September I'm riding a bike in the park when I meet this guy, also on a bicycle. I allow him to pick me up. He suggests we go somewhere for a drink. I suggest the most elegant place I know, the bar of the Stanhope Hotel.

We spend the afternoon together. I can't remember what we talk about because the entire time I'm thinking about the evening and how I will say no, push him away, or slam the door. I'm planning for the inevitable attack.

We get rid of the rented bikes and pick up his car. Then we go out for dinner. It's getting treacherous now because I realize he's investing a lot of money in me. After dinner he takes me to this really sleazy bar where there are a lot of blacks, a couple of hookers, and a few dykey women. Maybe he thinks the atmosphere will turn me on. At last he gets to the point "Let's go back to my place." I say, "No." But obviously I don't say no convincingly enough because I notice he's driving in the direction of his apartment and talking about what he can pick up for breakfast.

The thing is, I kind of like him because he's good-looking and he fits into my fantasies and I would like to have someone to date. All I want is a relationship. I'm not into the marriage bag at all. With me, it's more the Brenda Starr trip. But I don't want to sleep with him yet. First I'd like to know him and have him know me. So I keep repeating no.

Finally he proposes that he take me back to my apartment to get my pajamas and I should come home with him anyway. "Just to sleep," he promises, "and we'll go to Jones Beach first thing tomorrow morning."

Just call me Goldilocks. Schmuck that I am, I believe. I'm always looking for that one guy who is maybe a good guy. At his place I get undressed in the bathroom. I admit, I'm a little nervous but I'm having my period and I figure that will save me. As it turns out, the only one who cares is me. Not only hadn't I fucked much before, but I certainly had never fucked when I had my period.

Anyway, I brush my teeth and get into my Dr. Dentons. I had made sure the pajamas weren't sexy. God forbid I should look sexy but I feel a bit ambivalent here. I want him to think me attractive but not attractive enough to fuck. Or rape.

Johnny Carson is on. We get into bed. I say good night and turn on my side. My eyelids are closed but my eyes are wide open. Pretty soon I hear him turn off the TV and then the light. A minute later I feel a hand but I don't move because I'm supposed to be asleep.

Now I can't quite recall what happened next because somewhere along the line, I must have slipped into my old pattern with men. Meaning that I allow him to slide his hand into my pants and masturbate me. In a way I'm kind of digging it because I'm supposed to be asleep and can't be responsible anyway. Before long he's really getting into it and, at that point, I decide it's time to wake up. And I am enraged. *I jump out of bed screaming like a maniac, "I'M GOING HOME! I NEVER SHOULD HAVE COME HERE IN THE FIRST PLACE! THIS IS IT! GOODBYE!"*

There are two levels to my anger. For one, I am genuinely enraged at his breaking his promise. And then I have to act mad because supposedly I've just woken up to find his hand in my pants. I'm not lying because he's broken his word and whether I had allowed him to do it or not is of no consequence.

I put on my coat. He runs around saying, "No, no, no. Let's sit down and talk about this." I begin to feel terrible now. I think, "Maybe he really doesn't understand. Maybe he really wants to know how I feel."

We talk for about an hour until I decide I was right about him in the first place. At 4 a.m. I go outside and look for a cab.

When I get home, I am never so relieved in my whole life. Let me tell you.

V. LOVE GAMES

Meaningful Relationships. "Man's love is of man's life a thing apart; 'Tis woman's whole existence."

It took a man, in this case Byron, to come up with an idea like that.

While men are busy running the world, they prefer women to be constructively occupied with some all-consuming task. To ward off incipient cases of idle hands getting into mischief, they finally came up with a full-time occupation for us: Loving. Not just loving any old body but loving one of them, clearly an example of the most blatant self-interest.

From early childhood, a woman is aware of her duty to learn man-loving. However, her experiences with Daddy soon teach her the difficulties of the assignment, fascism being a poor breeding ground for genuine affection. This is not to suggest that a woman is incapable of love. On the contrary, the intense human impulse to care for others has not been wrung out of her as it has from men. Luckily, she remains an emotional primitive.

The catch is her obligation to love a man. By now she's agonized her way through a number of experiences where, against her better judgment, she committed herself heart and soul to loving a man and for her trouble got kicked in the teeth or pregnant. *She* was willing to accept love as her whole existence but, Byron bedamned, she secretly expected the man to do likewise.

Once she recognizes man's limited capacity for love and sees that his idea of love bears not the slightest resemblance to hers, she stops mucking about with romantic fantasies and starts to play the action-packed game of Loving. Meaning that while she pretends to abandon herself to emotion, she shrewdly withholds as much of herself as is necessary for self-preservation and her future financial security. Since marriage is the biggest business deal she'll ever negotiate, she can't be distracted by an enervating proposition like genuine love.

No welfare benefits being provided for those who can't find wifely work, she must locate a man to marry. It's equally clear that she must convince the man she loves him. In the good old days, a woman was able to marry without feigning unbridled passion but, too bad, those days are gone. Now it's even gauche to announce she's looking for a job. Men pretend to be more wary than ever, some having been known to dodge the ancient shotgun wedding ploy by pulling an abortionist out of their address books. This being the situation, a woman must exercise an unusually high degree of tact. The safest games are Meaningful Relationship and Living Together in which she pretends to reject marriage as a possible lifestyle.

> *Marriage Applicant: Marriage is for the birds. No sir, I'd rather be a comptometer operator at the Acme Hammock Company for the rest of my life than rot in a lousy marriage like my parents have. All I want is a meaningful relationship with a guy. If I loved a man, and the relationship worked out, then maybe I'd consider living together."*
> *Employer: "Right on, baby."*

Meaningful Relationship and Living Together are, of course, code names for Engagement and Marriage. While they may suggest temporary situations, that's precisely why they're such useful smoke screens. Invariably, Meaningful Relationship becomes an instructive game for a woman because she learns the truth about male concepts of love. Take the definition of the word "meaningful." To her, it implies a serious, committed kind of caring which goes beyond the physical. And maybe marriage. Diane discovered that Jerry was reading a different dictionary:

> *I met him on a vacation in the Catskills. He was a very sweet guy, really nice, and I thought that in many ways, we were similar. I sensed there was a real possibility for a relationship.*
>
> *But before long I realized he was only interested in me for sex. I was horny, too, but that wasn't all I was after. I tried discussing it with him. "Jerry," I said, "all our conversations end in fucking." In fact, I was really more upset than I let on. When we'd be out at dinner, my stomach would knot up because I'd be thinking, "Oh God, we're going to have to go home and fuck."*
>
> *When I tried to explain this to him, he thought I was asking for some sort of commitment. "Do you want me to stop seeing other girls?" was his question.*
>
> *So the relationship ended.*

Living Together, the game a woman sometimes must play before she can get married, is even more educational. One of its unexpected blessings is that she can test-market the man. If by some calamitous act of God, she finds him a one hundred percent irredeemable pig, she is free to pack her Ortho case and move out without benefit of attorney. Or throw him out, as Linda did. After four months of having Willy as a house guest, she suspected that Living Together could be a perilous adventure. However, that doesn't mean she isn't ready to try again:

> *If there are any healthy men around, I think perhaps I could live with one. But there are only five in New York. The experience taught me something: As many problems as I have, men have more. Whenever I'd try to talk about something personal, Willy would have an attack. He could talk about his job and books and sports but not about himself. Blah, blah, blah. What a bore his conversation was. Men simply aren't whole people; something has been left out or lost. Living with Willy showed me what a wonderful, together person I really am.*
>
> *He considered me inferior. How do I know? He told me. He's Jewish and he really believes women are inferior. Here we were, living together, and he never introduced me to his friends. If he wanted to see them, he'd say, "Well, I'm going out this evening. Bye." On the weekends, he'd fail to mention he was going away until the last minute. If he had forewarned me, I could have made plans with my friends. My conclusion was that he must have wanted me home alone.*
>
> *Sex was awful. The first time I didn't have an orgasm, which was soon after the relationship began, I told him so. "Oh well," he said, "that's not my fault." I mumbled in agreement. After that, I faked them. He was extremely rapid, a premature*

> *ejaculator, I guess, and I was just as glad. He said that he had a closer relationship with me than with anyone before. You can imagine how sick he must have been because he had no relationship with me.*
>
> *Living with Willy became so depressing, I got so mad that I started to eat. If I hadn't asked him to leave, I would have wound up a* real *mess.*

Living Together serves another important purpose: It jogs a woman's memory. Just in case she's forgotten Mother's domestic coolie games, she's quickly reminded of the real meaning of the word "housewife." Denise lived with Barney for a year before they married. Her experience can be considered the saga of an apprentice:

> *When I first met him, he had a lovely apartment off Gramercy Park. I loved to go over there after work. Because his work hours were from midnight to eight a.m., he'd be sleeping when I arrived. At the beginning he got up to open the door and make us coffee. Soon he gave me a key so that I could let myself in and he'd ask me to make the coffee. I'd serve it on a tray with a bowl of sugar. Finally he said, "Why don't you just put the sugar in while you're out in the kitchen?" See how slowly you get sucked in?*
>
> *When I moved in, I made a big mistake: I gave him the idea I could cook. At the beginning though, we went out for dinner all the time until he complained it was too expensive. I should have said, "Tough. I'll find another guy who can afford it." Or, "I'll pay for my own dinner." Or, at the very least, "Let's eat home and I'll make the chicken and you make the rice."*
>
> *But I didn't. I cooked.*
>
> *I didn't want him to feel threatened. He was very attracted to me and I wanted the love. I cooked*

> *and waited on him because these were the things a woman did when she wanted a relationship. Otherwise, you weren't a giving woman.*

And what happens to a giving woman? Like Denise, she gets married.

Wedding. At long last, Little Darling achieves her life's goal: owning a man of her own. After all those years of skulduggery, her rush to nowhere ends, and she can be Queen for a Day at Daddy's expense. That tradition should expect Daddy to finance the splendidly baroque game of Wedding seems to be a case of poetic justice. Even though she has spent the last quarter of a century administering a royal shakedown, so disturbing were the side effects that at times it hardly seemed worth the effort. Now that she has won a reprieve from Daddy's police state, she certainly feels entitled to nail him for a \$2,000, \$5,000, or \$15,000 wedding.

In the immortal words of a Long Island wedding caterer, "A bride should have (sic) respect." Ironically, her wedding day will be the only day in her life when she needn't have respect, not for the male establishment anyway. What's more, it is the one day when she can count on getting respect from men and be able to receive it standing up. The other occasions will be the births of her children, but then she'll be flat on her back, agonizing over her stitches.

Making the most of her one-day reign, she completely ignores the entire male sex, bridegroom included. As the invisible man, her future husband has a single function: to show up at the foot of the aisle and speak as few words as possible. Otherwise, he should be awed into speechlessness by the day's female pageantry and shut up for once.

Daddy's water is temporarily shut off, too. Rendered tongueless by the overpowering bills for chopped liver and Greek meatballs, he empties his savings account and joins the stand-up comedy routine at the altar to give away the bride.

Although he may be transferring his property to another member of the ruling sex, the joke is on them, for he deeds the bridegroom a painful case of sore testicles.

To the bracing strains of *Lohengrin,* Daddy's Little Darling gives a last-minute flip through Mother's homemade castration recipes, grabs her bouquet of baby's breath, and parades down the aisle bedecked as, of all things, a virgin.

FIVE

Everybody Ought to Have a Wife (Women Included)

I. NEWLYWED GAMES
- The First Hundred Days
- The Wife's Pledge of Allegiance

II. PARLOR GAMES
- Civil War
- The Wife-Beating Tapes
- The Real Meaning of Nagging

III. HOUSEKEEPING GAMES
- The Real Meaning of Taking Out the Garbage

IV. MONEY GAMES
- Butter Bread
- Pocket Money
- Just Helping Out, Thank You

V. BEDTIME GAMES
- How Marriage Ruined My Sex Life
- How to Drive a Husband to Infidelity Without His Ever Suspecting
- The Double Standard Revisited

VI. BABY GAMES
- Glorious Motherhood
- The Case of the Missing Daddy

Everybody Ought to Have a Wife (Women Included)

By divine right, a man is entitled to regard his home as his castle. But a castle isn't complete without a wife, the *little* woman destined from birth to create a Good Housekeeping Seal-of-Approval hideaway where he can escape the savage rigors of the office. Someone who will spend her life providing full restaurant and maid service, massaging his ego, raising his children, and, if time permits, paying daily homage to the Head of the Household. In return, she expects nothing but room and board. To get this terrific bargain, all a man must do is marry.

But while marriage is the perfect solution to a man's maintenance problem, it's the beginning of a woman's career as an indentured servant. If home is his castle, it's her forced labor camp, wall-to-wall Bigelowed though it may be. As a result, marriage is the battle for which women devise their most diabolical games.

This chapter may put husbands in a bad mood. Let's hope so.

I. NEWLYWED GAMES

The First Hundred Days. Little Darling, the former whatshername, inaugurates her new post by making a spot analysis of the power situation. Dedicated to the proposition that there can be only one boss—it may not be her, but it's sure as hell not going to be him—she applies herself to winning the crucial struggle for leadership. When her husband isn't looking, she begins bit by bit to whittle away at his testicles. No matter what she thinks about the ethics of such an underhanded tactic, it does have style. In any case, she has no choice.

Despite the care she has taken to marry a man susceptible to management, she still must face a jolting reality: Marriage is set up, take it or leave it, as a master-slave relationship. No man voluntarily settles for anything less than running things. Indeed, he insists upon it. For if there is one thing he dreads, it's a woman with sufficient power to dominate him, or, ghastly memories of his mother, a woman capable of walloping the shit out of him.

As far as he's concerned, marriage is a safe harbor where he can fulfill his anatomical destiny by assuming the full privileges of male supremacy. Anything short of being top dog, including an equal relationship with his wife, would diminish his manliness. Although a wife fails to see the logic of this nonsense, she puts on a good show of acquiescence. Bearing in mind the mythology about women which never fails to beguile men, she overwhelms him with three robust lies:

1. She's delighted to serve him.
2. She'll accept second place without sulking.
3. She's satisfied to live vicariously from now on.

As the old-fashioned inspirational bilge goes, for richer or for poorer, for better or for worse. Rich or poor depends on him, though; she's merely along for the ride. It's a disconcerting thought.

To her consternation, she begins to half-believe the myths about her sex. Since her husband desperately wishes to believe them, reinforcing her image as a cheerful lackey requires little thought. With a sense of *deja vu,* she reaches back to her formative years for mother's highly successful game, that oldtimer, Lawd, Miz Scarlett, I Doan Know Nuthin Bout Birthin Babies. It runs roughly like this: more or less submissive, she impersonates the old family retainer he expects as his due. Naturally, she shuffles. The rest of the stereotype—eagerness to please, helplessness, childishness, admiration and awe for her betters—is a cinch. Put them all together and you've got your dependable Dependent. Or so her husband believes. Doesn't it say so on his W-2 form?

But perfecting Lawd, Miz Scarlett is only part of the madness facing a new wife. At the same time, she must suppress her instinct to back out of what is clearly an overrated lifestyle. Marriage, another bright idea from the wonderful people who gave us bound feet, is obviously an imbecilic existence for a woman. She takes whatever measures seem necessary for the maintenance of her sanity.

A therapeutic beginning is to leave $75 of her new husband's money at the Super Giant where she fuels up on staples no kitchen should be without: instant coffee, presugared cereals, precooked vegetables, heat-and-serve everythings. No sense overdoing the games. At the checkout counter she picks up the latest issue of *Woman's Day* to see if there's a recipe for the contemporary version of mother's specialty, meat loaf anointed with Campbell's Tomato Soup. There is: meatballs anointed with Campbell's Cream of Mushroom Soup, otherwise known as beef stroganoff. Unfortunately, she must add sour cream, a bothersome innovation doubtless reflecting *Woman's Day's* salute to the new, more highly educated generation of housewives.

The fact that during her single days she would have turned up her nose at such a vile concoction is beside the point. Thanks to the frogs' legs *provencale* and *peche* Melbas supplied by Some Other Woman's Husband, plus the pastrami sandwiches courtesy of dates, and her own home-cooked dinners of ninety-nine percent fat-free yogurt, she managed to eat fairly high on the hog. Now that producing daily meals is her worry, she will sit down to inedible casseroles she wouldn't have touched before.

In fact, from here on in, she begins to do a lot of unimaginable things. And why not? She is no longer herself. Forfeiting her name might seem a trivial matter but, having had it for twenty or twenty-five years, she had grown attached. However, she is compensated for the loss of whatever slight identity she once had by a new, masculine name, Mrs. John Whatshisname.

Thus armed with a secret alias, and the psychological freedom of an anonymous person, she becomes a wrecking crew of one. The target scheduled for demolition: her husband's monumental ego and his absurd lust for power. If she hadn't calculated on getting her quota of control, she wouldn't have married him in the first place. Obviously this information can't be allowed to fall into his hands. Therefore, concurrently with Lawd, Miz Scarlett, she must play another of her mother's basic games, Conspiracy. Its underlying premise is the old Anglo-Saxon concept that a person cannot be compelled to testify against herself. Claiming immunity against self-incrimination, she publicly declares that marriage is nifty while privately sharing her heresies with those who know better. Women.

For example, it may not be gallant to say so, but when women speak to other women about *why* they married the men they did, the word love is heard only accidentally:

> *AMANDA - Around the age of twenty-four I went through an intensely rebellious period which was self- destructive in many ways. The most self-destructive thing I did was to marry Leo.*

> *DENISE - When I graduated, I got a job paying $85 a week, lived in a cheap apartment, and tried to work my way up in my job. I couldn't go on living that sort of deprived existence, so I married a man ten years older, one who had a certain amount of status and was already established in his work. At the same time, I made sure he wasn't a go-getter because I wanted the spotlight. Barney didn't seem to mind if the attention was focused on me. I never looked at marriage romantically in that I wasn't interested in boys my own age. They could have been drafted.*

NORA - The only men I met were these arrogant Brahmin types who killed themselves to show how much more than me they knew. I was fed up with so-called intellectuals. Roy had a tiny brain. He was refreshingly simpleminded. I figured I could get along with him because he wouldn't give me a hard time. I was wrong.

JUDY - Carl reminded me of my father. Unfortunately, at that time I didn't fully realize what a schmuck my father really was.

DEBORAH - Except for the maternal feelings I have for my children, love is a meaningless word. At the time I married, I was an overgrown adolescent. Love meant somebody paying attention to me. Even now, I don't know what love is. I know what screwing is.

LEAH - He was charming, self-assured, and attractive. At first he took care of himself but gradually he grew fat and went bald very fast. Ten years ago I thought he was a person I'd like to spend my life with. I'm not sure if I loved him.

FELICIA - I was pregnant.

Paramount among a good wife's qualities is loyalty. Never questioning that he owns a good wife, a husband refuses to believe she tattles on him. Nor does he suppose her capable of concealing her feelings. Touchdown for our side. Protected by his illusion that children and other subordinates are constitutionally unable to hide their thoughts from a perceptive superior, a wife can confidently settle down to working at her marriage. By now, she hopes, the opposition is badly disorganized.

The Wife's Pledge of Allegiance.

I WILL make my husband feel like a king by waiting on him hand and foot.

I WILL never reveal that he farts in bed.

I WILL butter his toast, make his bed, Ivory-Snow his socks, and buy his Gillette Platinum-Plus's because this is as it should be.

I WILL never compete, only complement.

I WILL try and remember to jump when he says jump.

I WILL never disclose that the B'nai B'rith bowling league knows he's impotent.

I WILL fulfill myself by producing children, the most creative work a woman can do.

I WILL use my B.A. in art history to make my husband and children happy.

I WILL Stanislavski my techniques for faking orgasms and never blame him because I'm frigid.

I WILL pollute my body with hormones, chemicals, and steel coils so that he can enjoy carefree sex.

I WILL hide my collection of dirty books and my vibrator, and masturbate when he's at the office.

I WILL never challenge his cock-and-bull story that a man's work must be taken seriously.

I WILL remind myself not to laugh convulsively when he complains what a tough day he's had at the office.

I WILL listen sympathetically to tales of his mother's misdeeds and suppress my temptation to take her side; I will take over the job of writing his letters to her.

I WILL smile inscrutably when he calls me stupid in the presence of his friends, my parents, and our children.

I WILL never pass him the women's page and keep the news section for myself.

I WILL display jubilation when he remembers my birthday with a General Electric Toast-R-Oven.

I WILL never admit that I hate to cook.

I WILL silently accept the blame for moving to the suburbs.

I WILL thank him for helping out on those memorable occasions when he changes a Pamper, washes a dish, or empties an ash tray.

I WILL, if necessary, take a part-time clerical job to help out the family finances, but when the children get chicken pox, I will never ask him to take the day off.

I WILL never condemn him for purchasing a Honda when he reaches the male menopause.

I WILL bite my tongue when he beefs about marriage being a raw deal for men.

ACHTUNG!

II. PARLOR GAMES

Civil War. One of the most baffling facts a new wife notices about her mate is his conspicuous, uncharacteristic silence. Unlike the courtship when he was either advising how she should run her life, or reporting the latest news about himself and his mother, now he is ominously quiet. After years of playing Listening and Keeping One's Mouth Shut, she suddenly finds there is no man to listen *to*.

Although it's too soon to be sure, she gets the uncomfortable feeling that he's disinterested in her. When Angela's marriage was six weeks old, she faced just such a domestic political crisis:

> *One night he came home and announced it was time for him to, as he put it, "get involved in the community."*
>
> *"Wait a minute," I said. "What does that mean?" Well, he planned to volunteer as a campaign worker for a congressional candidate. It would involve three evenings a week. "The hell you are," I thought to myself. However, I couldn't say it. How could I have objected to his being such a civic-minded guy?*

What I did was stop speaking to him for a week. Slowly he began to get the message until finally he said, "I mentioned my plan to Mother and she said, 'Won't Angela be lonely?'" He guessed as how Mother might be right. He guessed. The turd.

I won that one.

Periodically the freeze lifts when one of his cronies drops by to shoot the breeze, but otherwise, he escapes behind the newspaper. And if it isn't the paper, it's television, office homework, or naps. Four wives profile the man who stopped talking:

THE GO-GETTER (NORA'S MAN) - During the year we dated, he spent every evening running from bar to bar, party to party. He was a big playboy who never spent an evening at home. Then we got married and all of a sudden, whammo, every night he comes home with his attache case stuffed full of crap. "Got to work tonight," he'd announce. After turning on the TV, he'd strew the junk all over the living room floor. Every so often, he'd move a paper from one pile to another or scribble a memo. But I could see he wasn't accomplishing a thing. It was an act to avoid talking to me.

THE SLEEPER (GLORIA'S MAN) - He uses sleep as an escape. "I'm tired," he says. Well, what about me? I've worked hard all day, too. Still, I would like to do something in the evenings, if only talk.

He's a limited person. When he comes home from work, he goes directly to the liquor cabinet and makes himself a martini. When we were first married, I used to mix it, with a twist of lemon no less, and chill it in the freezer. I must have been out of my bloody mind. Anyway, he takes his drink out on the porch and waits until he hears me announce dinner. Then he comes into the kitchen to bug me about what kind of wine we're drinking with the meal. Frankly, I don't give a shit but every night he makes a big thing about it. He'll lift the lids off the pots to see what's cooking: "Gloria, I really don't think this Portuguese rose is right for shrimp. Why didn't you buy a Chablis or at least a white Bordeaux?"

Okay, so then we eat. By dessert, he can hardly keep his eyes open. After dinner he adjourns to the living room where he turns on the TV and falls asleep five minutes later. For years I used to wonder, "What is he thinking? What is he feeling?" The answer is not a damn thing.

THE TUBE-SUCKER (ANGELA'S MAN) - *The goddam TV became my chief rival. When I'd say something to him, he might answer or he might not. But if he did, he never took his eyes off the screen. He wouldn't look at me. The only time I could be sure he was listening was during the commercials. And some commercials were more fascinating than me. It was like living with a zombie. After hours trying to get his attention, sometime I'd get desperate and yell, "Let's talk."*

"Okay," he'd say, "What do you want to talk about?" By that time, I was so mad I couldn't think of a thing to say. I mean, shouldn't conversation come naturally?

THE GRABBER (DEBORAH'S MAN) - *I try to talk to him. He doesn't seem to understand that I need conversation with an adult on some other subject than the kids or things that must be done around the house. Yet I can't have a discussion with him on an adult level without his interpreting it as a sexual overture. If I talk about politics or books or music, even if I'm washing dishes, somehow it*

> *winds up with him grabbing me when that's the farthest thing from my mind.*
>
> *I have considered not speaking to him at all but that's very difficult for me. And yet if I do try to involve him in a conversation, I know what's going to happen.*
>
> *Certain times are safe. For example, at the dinner table the kids are present.*

Over and over again, she relentlessly tries to break through the communications barrier and open negotiations. Because even if he doesn't have anything to say, she does. Plenty. She pushes for discussion in two key areas:

1. Herself, meaning the standard injustices which accompany the position of wife.
2. Him, meaning exhortations to straighten up and fly right.

However, the last thing she wishes to do is provoke a rumpus. With a minimum of dramatics she plays it safe with Don't Rock the Boat, an offensive game whose political implications aren't difficult to unravel:

> *Wife: "Darling, if you're going to be late for dinner, I wish you'd call and let me know."*
> *Husband: "I forget."*
> *Wife: "It only takes a dime to call."*
> *Husband: "What are you trying to do? Control me?"*
> *Wife: "...."*

Don't Rock the Boat allows her to live in peace while at the same time cautiously bringing complaints out into the open and, thereby, maybe improving the atmosphere of domestic relations. Parlaying with her women friends may be therapeutic, but it does nothing to change the relationship with her husband which is inadequate, in her opinion.

However, protocol demands that she restrain herself. The alternative, escalation of hostilities, is too hazardous. She doesn't dare fight at full strength because, in an unguarded moment, she might honestly reveal what's on her mind. The other reason she avoids straight shooting in fights is that rebellion provokes her husband's anger. While he may react initially to a domestic uprising with benevolent attention to grievances, ultimately the insurgent must be put down. Simply due to the fact that a husband is heavier, the threat of physical retaliation is always present. Leah's husband wouldn't hurt a fly:

> *As long as I agreed with him, everything went along hunky-dory. But the minute I expressed an opinion contrary to his, pffft. It wasn't until after we married that I discovered he had a vicious temper. Later, he became completely unbearable. But he wasn't one of those husbands who would hit his wife.*

And then there are the husbands who *would* hit their wives.

The Wife-Beating Tapes

> *THE SWINGER - I can go just so far before he starts swinging. But it took me several years to find that out.*
>
> *Since the time he fractured my jaw, I've been extremely careful. It happened one evening when we were entertaining some of his friends from the clinic, doctors and their wives. All of our friends are his friends. I had spent two days preparing for this dinner party, a big production with Chateaubriand and chocolate mousse and God knows what. By the end of the evening, I was exhausted and had a splitting headache.*

When the guests left, he went into the bathroom and I could hear him brushing his teeth and getting ready for bed. Somehow he didn't notice the six million dirty dishes and pots which he expected me to take care of. "Listen, you bastard," I yelled, "I don't intend to stay up half the night. Help me clean up." I was so tired and infuriated, I was past caring what I said. I told him his friends were bores and I was tired of waiting on them and then being treated as a charwoman. He didn't like that a bit.

When he got through with me, I was lying next to the refrigerator. I couldn't move. I remember laying there for a long time until the pain in my jaw became excruciating and I got up to fix an ice pack.

When I told him I had to see a doctor, he wouldn't let me go. He examined me himself and said I was exaggerating. The real reason was, he was afraid one of his colleagues would recognize his name. It wouldn't look good for a doctor's wife to say she'd been beaten by her husband. It might hurt his professional reputation.

Someday, when the children are older, I'll leave him. Or kill him.

THE SMASHER - The first time it happened was three or four months after we married. I was shocked because I didn't dream this sweet, easygoing little fellow would smash anybody in the face. So the next day when he didn't refer to the incident, I thought maybe I'd imagined it He acted as if nothing had happened.

A couple of months later, he got sore over a sock I'd lost at the laundromat, and we started to fight, and the next thing I knew, my face was bloody. He walked out and didn't come home until after I was asleep. The next day he didn't want to talk about it. Neither did I.

However, after several years I was determined to make a stink because I didn't think I could go on living with him. When I cornered him, all he would say was, "We don't make love enough." Interesting, he believes there are two ways for a man to release his tensions: screwing and violence. If he didn't fuck me, then he would have to beat me. In any case, it was my fault.

I'll say this for him: He never hit me when I was pregnant. Those were the only times in six years that I've felt safe. I guess he was afraid of hurting the baby.

He beat me up in front of Anne when she was eleven months old. At the sight of the blood, she became terrified and started to scream. I felt so humiliated that my child witnessed this that 1 insisted we go to a marriage counselor. Actually, I wanted him to see a psychiatrist. "You're sick," I said. "You have a problem." When he rejected that idea, I suggested we both should get help, like it was my fault and he'd be doing me a favor. I found a therapist, made the appointment, and he dragged along.

The three counseling sessions were hysterical. At the outset, the doctor mentioned that our problem was by no means unusual. Many husbands beat their wives. I guess that was meant to make me feel good. At first my husband kept his mouth shut; when he did talk, he started on his sex deprivation theory and spent the whole session whining about how he didn't get enough and what was he to do with a frigid wife. At the second session, he and the doctor were getting pretty buddy-buddy. The doctor started to work on my sex problems. By the third session, I was determined to discuss the real reason we were there: that my husband expressed his anger by pummel ing me half to death. "Look, doctor," I recall saying, "he beat me up in the presence of Anne. Don't you think this was unwise?" Yes, the doctor did. But the gist of his advice was that my husband should control himself around the child. Apparently beating me up at other times was okay. Incredible!

I could see the therapy was useless, so I never made another appointment. The only good thing to come out of it was that my husband stopped hitting me in front of the children.

THE PUNCHER - *He only punches me when he drinks. The rest of the time, he's fine. Unfortunately his drinking has steadily increased during the past sixteen years. So have the beatings.*

I have to be careful when he comes home from work. Frequently he'll stop off for a couple of drinks with the guys from the office. If he's not home by eight, it means he's had three or four drinks and I'd better cool it when he walks in the door because he's looking for trouble. Once he showed up for dinner at 10:30. I was furious. "Your dinner is on the stove," I said. "Heat it up yourself." He looked at the pork chops which, I admit, looked like shit by then and threw the frying pan at me. "Do you expect me to eat this garbage?" That incident ended with me getting a black eye and not going out for a week.

Parties are the worst. If I so much as go over and stand next to him, he'll say, "Circulate." He gets paranoid because he thinks I'm counting his drinks. If I look at him sideways, he says I'm spoiling his fun. He's a terrible show-off at parties anyway and by the end of the evening he's unbearable. If I show my disapproval, he becomes enraged and starts pushing me and then punching at my breasts and stomach. He says I bring it on myself because if I didn't make him feel self-conscious, he wouldn't get mad.

The Real Meaning of Nagging. There are dozens of ways to castrate a husband, but most of them involve knives. One which does not is Nagging, a game of unilateral harassment which achieves several important political objectives:

1. Expression of serious grievances.
2. Dismemberment of the husband's ego.

Nagging also permits a wife to step out of line and twist her husband's short hairs. Which reminds April of Sunday school:

> *The first woman God created was Lilith who refused to take the recumbent position in intercourse. When Adam tried to rape her, she got so mad that she screwed a demon and produced a lot of evil spirits to haunt the world.*
>
> *Then Eve comes along and says to Adam, "Sure, okay baby, you can climb on top of me." Since she's a good lady, she cheerfully allows him to schtook her from above every night. Meanwhile, that bitch Lilith is creating all sorts of troubles for the world.*
>
> *The story is a warning to every husband: Don't let your wife get out of hand. Don't let her take the superior position. Or your troubles are going to multiply.*
>
> *That's why men are always wary when they suspect a wife is stepping out of line.*

Nagging throws him off the track because it appears to involve insignificant complaints. For example:

> *Nagger: "For the last time, hang your wet towel in the bathroom. It doesn't belong on the bedroom floor."*
> *Husband: "I've got more important things on my mind in the mornings."*

And off he meanders to his office, bolstered by the notion that the little woman must spend her day drinking coffee and dreaming up trivial complaints. Besides, doesn't she have all day to pick up his towels and dirty underwear which is, after all, her job in the first place? So what's she bitching about anyway?

It's safe to state, without qualification, that Nagging is never based on trivia. On the contrary, Nagging reflects her chronic revulsion to women's place which entails, among other things, personal valet service. Since she finds it inexplicable that a mature human being should actually expect such service—*she* doesn't—she takes the necessary measures to achieve her long-term mission: slashing him down to size. The area in which she can impose the most cutting wounds is in bed. Nagging merely picks at the scabs.

III. HOUSEKEEPING GAMES

The Real Meaning of Taking Out the Garbage. Far from appreciating his wife's domestic services, a husband regards them as his right. Oddly enough, he behaves as if he has been accustomed to a maid.

He has.

His mother.

Weary of stepping and fetching, desperate for help, Mother recruited Little Darling the moment she could hold a dish cloth. She gave up on little brother who, recognizing a bad deal when he saw it, demonstrated his total lack of aptitude. Even when it came to caring for his own body, he showed noticeable backwardness. While Little Darling was fully toilet trained by the age of two, brother wore diapers until three or later with the blessings of the Dr. Spocks who assured mother *all* little boys were like that.

By the time he marries, he still can barely wipe himself, but now he knows the reason: Men were destined for important work. The rest is better left for lesser folks. In other words, his wife, who has the mentality for housework and valet service. She doesn't mind. In fact, she likes it.

And if she doesn't, she obliges anyway. Gloria couldn't

solve the riddle which has plagued housewives for millions of years: Since a husband works, how can he be expected to do housework, too?

> *For ten years he's sat at the table after dinner without lifting a finger. He pushes his plate away, crumples his napkin, and throws it aside. If it falls to the floor, that's okay. He doesn't notice. Then he lights one of his filthy cigars and sits there puffing like a self-content, obese hog.*
>
> *He doesn't notice the two-step I'm doing between the kitchen and the dining room, hauling away the dirty plates, making coffee, bringing in the dessert, filling up the dishwasher. He never moves. He never offers to help.*
>
> *For many years I've wanted to scream and bash him over the head with the dishes. But I have never been able to say the unspeakable: Get off your ass and* do something."

It's not easy for a woman to accept the bizarre ideology that housework is her destiny. However, as Denise's struggle demonstrates, even the most unwilling wife finally succumbs:

> *I was very hip. I was only going to live with him. Even though somehow I got roped into cooking, that didn't mean I was willing to do housework. Before we married, he agreed to wash dishes. His apartment had a dishwasher. Then we married and moved to an apartment without a dishwasher. Suddenly he didn't want the dishwashing job anymore.*
>
> *I refused to clean. Dust began to pile up. The only thing I cleaned was myself; I took a bath every day.*
>
> *Then, because he was supporting me, I decided to stop working for a while. He told me, "I support you. You should clean the house." Okay, I thought, and proceeded to do the whole housewife number,*

> *including the steak with wine sauce and mushrooms. Once a week I had a cleaning woman and what she didn't do, I cleaned myself. And before I knew it, I was saying to myself, "Well, while I'm at home, maybe I'll have a baby." So I got pregnant.*

Since she can't figure out a logical reason for unloading the housework on him, she approaches the subject obliquely. Even though she may go along with the unsettling fact that men like her husband have usurped the universe, she wants some small part of the world to be her domain. She takes the only unoccupied territory, the kitchen, where she proceeds to throw her weight around by drafting a few slave laborers of her own.

If a wife is determined enough, she can shame her husband into "helping out." As it turns out, her standard request—taking out the garbage—happens to be wonderfully symbolic. Her sex, of course, has been designated caretaker of the world's garbage. The wife in particular vows to spend her life cleaning up messes. Collecting trash is one thing; disposing of it is the last straw, the lowest job of all. What could be more gratifying than the honorable Head of the Household hauling away the rubbish she has collected?

Delegation of other household chores such as dishwashing holds less satisfaction and demands far more intimidation. Surprisingly, a husband rarely quibbles about assuming responsibility for the garbage. He may balk at the dishes. The problem here is that a moron could do a fairly adequate job of garbage disposal, but the dishes should be clean. And, like every task she assigns, he turns in a spectacularly lousy performance in the hope that she will scrap her idea. Roberta explains the exasperating dilemma:

> *Now John does the dishes regularly. But one minute I'm yelling, "John, get in the kitchen and do the dishes," and the next I'm screaming, "What are you doing? You're getting water all over the place." It's the same thing when he helps with the baby. At the beginning we established that he would do his*

> *share. But since he does a lousy job of diapering, I find myself criticizing. I patiently show him over and over, "Now, this is the way you do it."*
>
> *I won't give up and do it all myself. I won't.*

While the old-fashioned husband reacts to sharing household chores by retreating behind machismo, the liberated husband appears more cooperative. If cornered, he will agree and hope his wife forgets about it tomorrow. When she remembers, he performs his assignment sloppily and anticipates a speedy reprieve. And if this is not forthcoming, he passes along his share of the work to a paid domestic. For example, request some men to empty the garbage, and they cough up $240 for a Hotpoint Garbage Compactor. Ask others to vacuum the living room, defrost the refrigerator, or clean the oven, and $15 a week magically appears for a cleaning woman. Chide them for leaving a ring around the tub, and they go back to taking showers.

Those who have made a cult of slovenliness still apparently feel duty bound to supervise the cleaning efforts of the other sex. Felicia's husband is an autocrat at the dinner table, so long as she does the work:

> *His standards are extremely high. He expects impeccable service at his house. A couple of times each summer I try to get away with paper plates by calling dinner a picnic. Without fail, he turns up his nose: "I can't eat off* this. *It leaks."*
>
> *If he had to wash dishes, we'd be eating from a trough.*

IV. MONEY GAMES

Butter Bread. There's no way around it: Little Darling is penniless. That marriage should automatically throw a woman into the pauper category is hardly accidental though. To discourage a mass exodus of runaways, the male establishment tries to make certain wives have no access to ready cash. As a further precaution, there's the unspoken warning that a woman who displeases The Breadwinner may find herself room-and-boardless. When a wife plays the face-saving game of Butter Bread, she assures her husband she can't possibly get along without him. For once, she's speaking the truth. Natalie considers what it would take to become a defector:

> *He knows he's got me. I have no choice but to stay with him because I can't support myself and three kids. Someday I may inherit money from my father, but the men in my family usually live to be ninety-nine.*
>
> *If I ever get my hands on money, my husband had better start worrying.*

To present the situation from a more positive standpoint, here's Mrs. Helen Andelin, founder of the Fascinating Womanhood Foundation:

> *When you cast your bread upon the waters, it comes back buttered.*

Playing Butter Bread means listening, without a single boo, to the standard oratory of The Breadwinner who is eternally noting:

> *Breadwinner: "Insurance is a rough way to earn a dollar, you'd better believe it."*
>
> *and/or*
>
> *Breadwinner: "You don't know how lucky you are to be able to stay home while I'm out killing myself for a buck. But a man has the responsibility for supporting his family."*

Why tamper with a man's sense of responsibility? Since he casts her as a lady of leisure or, at best, a laborer whose work is unimportant, she diligently exacts her revenge by spending his money. If The Breadwinner's earnings are adequate, there's a luscious opportunity to sublimate her creative juices at the local shopping center. Under the guise of making ends meet, she hunts down the most useless items she can find. As long as he thinks she has his best penny-pinching interests at heart, she can order wall-to-wall carpeting for the garage and plastic covers for the living room furniture with little fear of flak.

Even the wife with a meager income at her disposal can look forward to the sensual adventure of marketing because The Breadwinner likes to eat well. The sexual high point of her day is pushing her cart up and down the aisles of the housewife's brothel while fondling the chicken breasts and shamelessly masturbating the melons.

Contrary to their outward behavior, women are far from senseless about money. One reason a wife can be cavalier about The Breadwinner's wealth is, she suspects him of offering blood money. No matter how tight he may be, he must feel guilty about something or why would he allow her to spend it. If it were her money, she'd be a lot more careful. In fact, if she could help it, she wouldn't hand over her earnings to a man. Or, as in Yvette's case, do so cautiously:

> *In the beginning I had the money. All of it. I was working; he was going to school. I gave him, resentfully I admit, money to pay the bills. But I wanted him to use it sensibly. When he traded in our brand new Volkswagen for a four-year-old MG because he couldn't live without it, I thought, "Ridiculous." I acquiesced because he wanted the car but I didn't just hand over the money. I made him scrape.*
>
> *We didn't have a joint checking account. I would write him checks on my account to cover bills and his personal needs. I knew that if I gave him $5,000, he'd pay what we owed and blow the rest.*
>
> *Now that I no longer work, I still have to watch*

him. He's frivolous. For example, he got carried away about buying a bar for the patio. That's a purchase I could have lived without.

Those who rarely get their hands on a dollar know the value of it when they do. The fact that she is actually a far superior manager is normally not thrown in The Breadwinner's face. Deborah oversees the treasury in her family:

He wouldn't have a penny if it weren't for me but I don't let him know that. "How can we be in debt on my salary?" he moans. And yet if I'd let him, we'd be in the poor house. For example, he'll say, "Let's go out for dinner." Since there are five of us, this has to mean $20 or $25. "There's no need," I say. "Let's get pizza instead." But he wants to do it for me, to make me happy.

Every other month he complains about my spending. I tell him, "I'm not interested in your complaints." It irks me because he's the one who's disorganized about money. I always keep a reserve, either in cash or in the bank, because that's just sensible to me. To him, it's not. I would never let myself get down to a few cents in my pocket the way he does. "Ration your money," I say, "You don't need six drinks at lunch. What would you say if I blew the food money?" But he knows I won't.

Pocket Money. Not only is shopping a wife's chief erogenous pleasure, but it also provides a splendid opportunity to mangle The Breadwinner's ego. If aspersions on his virility is her Number One castration technique, then implying he's stingy ranks Number Two. Breadwinning is one of man's most fruitful ego trips, for he can't be a breadwinner unless someone consents to eat the bread. He wants a dependent, right? He gets one. Deliberately regressing back to childhood, his wife pretends he's Daddy and proceeds to rob him within the bounds of safety. At the same time she pays lip service to the preposterous myth that *his* money is *our* money. If ever she makes the mistake of believing it's *our* money, she finds out differently should they separate or divorce. Suddenly and mysteriously, *our* money is his.

But the still-married Breadwinner knows what's fair: Dependents deserve pocket money. Against his better judgment, because he knows women have no talent for math, he is moved to dole out an allowance. If he thinks her fairly intelligent, he encourages her own checking account. Roberta may be a doctoral candidate, but when it comes to her bank account, she gets that old childish feeling:

> *Throughout our marriage we've played this game: Periodically I get a notice from the bank that I'm overdrawn. And periodically I get out my stubs and my bank statement, and he straightens it out.*
>
> *He just thrives on my dependency. "You're just like a little girl," he says fondly when I fuck up over my bank account, because especially he digs my incompetency in areas which involve money. In the beginning of our marriage, it was clearly defined that I would go to school and he would take care of money, tax returns, insurance, in fact, anything which would be necessary for me to maintain and support myself.*
>
> *He thinks it's right-on for me to get a job because it would supplement our income. What he doesn't realize is, a meal ticket of my own would mean my ticket to independence.*

Deborah receives an allowance:

> *Every two weeks he gives me a lump sum in cash. I have twenty different envelopes: food, baby-sitters, the maid, bowling, piano lessons, junk. I*

> *take care of everything except the charge accounts and the mortgage payments. Never once in twelve years have I had to ask him for more money.*
>
> *What burns me up is that he borrows from me so often that I have an envelope marked Tony. He's always running short and asking me for lunch money because he doesn't reserve the amount he needs. Therefore, I never feel I'm getting my full allowance.*
>
> *Since I opened my own checking account and he can't get his hands on it, he bugs me less often. He knows it's a bloody battle to get a check out of me. I'd do anything not to give him money. Oh, he pays me back but I like to keep my account nice and orderly without having to make allowance for outstanding debts.*

Just Helping Out, Thank You. If a wife wants $500 a year of her own, she becomes an Avon Lady and assures The Breadwinner she's just helping out. If she wants $5,000, she takes a full-time job, but still acts like an Avon Lady because competition makes The Breadwinner twitchety.

Just Helping Out, Thank You is a game scarcely worth a woman's time or talent. She plays it, however, because there are a few undeniable advantages, money for one. She hoards as big a chunk of her salary as possible, for, while she may claim she's working to help out, the main person she wants to help is herself. A job is one way to find out if she can converse intelligently with grown-ups, something she seriously begins to doubt after years of non-conversations with The Breadwinner and semi-conversations with her kids. A job, of course, relieves her of twenty-four-hour-a-day child duty, and, for that reason alone, is worth considering. However, and here's the rub, if she imagined a job would spring her from the ranks of the forced labor crew, she soon discovers it only means a daily parole.

The Breadwinner: "Since you started working, the house looks like a pigsty. I come home to find the sink full of dirty dishes and the beds unmade."
Avon Lady: "I know, dear, but remember I'm working to help out."
The Breadwinner: "If you can't keep the house clean, you should quit."
Avon Lady: "Maybe you could make the beds."
The Breadwinner: "When I come home, I want to relax."

Just Helping Out means working two jobs instead of one. According to popular mythology, the working wife has no trouble managing two shifts. If she does, she should quit, the paid job that is. The unpaid one she must keep. Reluctant to admit she's not superhuman, she plugs ahead until either she collapses from physical fatigue or persuades The Breadwinner that part of her salary—never his—should be spent on a maid. Amanda and her husband were both painters. The story of how she became a casualty:

> *My husband made little money from his paintings and so when we were first married, Daddy contributed and then I took over the job of supporting us. Since I felt my earnings were mine, I wanted to open my own bank account. He thought this was terribly selfish of me.*
>
> *With his authoritarian view of the husband-wife relationship, naturally he wanted me to be subordinate and in the beginning I did look up to him. So when I was making most of the money, it just about killed him. For awhile I taught school and that he barely could accept. However, he certainly couldn't accept me as a painter; it was too much competition. He was the man; therefore, if anyone was going to be the artist in the family, it should be him. Eventually I stopped painting and began to study photography. I told myself that I must be*

realistic and work at something commercial so that I could make money. The real reason I switched was that I didn't want to compete with him.

After Karin was born, I found a job as a photographer's assistant. At that time my husband painted at home and, although he complained I was running away from the baby, he stayed with her while I was at work. Anyway, we couldn't afford a baby-sitter, not with the kind of bills he racked up. My salary couldn't cover the apartment and his truck and a baby-sitter. I wouldn't have minded supporting him except that he shit on me while I was doing it. He beat me down as a woman while he was spending my money. After we separated, it took me a year to get out of debt.

My job was physically exhausting. All day long I lugged around cameras and equipment, and stood for hours in the darkroom. When I came home, he expected me to cook and clean and shop and put the baby to bed. My whole life slowly became a nightmare.

I should have protested but I never did. It didn't occur to me. Also, I was afraid of his anger. But I knew I couldn't keep up the pace for very long.

Just Helping Out is an exceedingly depressing game if for no other reason than it means going back to a place from which she once escaped, The Office. One housekeeping job is bad enough; two would be unbearable. Rather than face another round of fetching for and serving The Boss and The Company Man, Little Darling searches for other means to weather her growing dejection.

V. BEDTIME GAMES

How Marriage Ruined My Sex Life. Okay, the Almighty didn't intend womankind to enjoy sex. After a third of a lifetime, a wife is convinced. As a child, it was secret masturbation; as an adolescent, manhandling by guys who didn't know where to put it; as a single young woman, locating a man who could get it up and keep it up. And now, after all those dismal years, marriage.

If she thought bachelors were bad about remembering the courtly preliminaries once they'd first scored, she finds that husbands automatically subscribe to the shortcut-theory-of-sex. She doesn't know what monotonous is until she's married.

Sooner than later, sex becomes profoundly boring and, finally, the biggest bane of her existence. Not unpredictably, she will devote more hours to devising stratagems for avoiding it than she will spend cooking or cleaning. Eloquent testimonials to the fact that marriage puts a crimp in a woman's sex life:

1. *"In any long-term relationship, married or not, sex with the same person becomes terribly boring. But since it's my duty, I really feel I should try. Personally, I'd like to have sex with him once every six months."*
2. *"I don't have a low sex drive, except with him. To keep our marriage peaceful, I cooperate once a week."*
3. *"It's okay that he thinks I'm cold because now he doesn't ask so often. He says I don't make enough effort. But if I do let myself go, I just wind up frustrated."*
4. *"The sex books imply there's something wrong with you if you don't want it all the time. Sex is not my primary interest and never has been. Less than a year after I married, the excitement wore off. Was I supposed to say, "Honey, you don't turn me on anymore?" When I hear women married ten or fifteen years claim they still enjoy sex with their husbands, I think, "Oh come off it. Who do you think you're kidding?"*
5. *"If I know he's going to want sex, I'll have*

a couple of brandies after dinner or take two Libriums."
6. *"I've managed to convince him that I don't have time for sex now because I'm too busy with my job."*
7. *"If the TV is on, I pay attention to Dick Cavett. Otherwise, I plan my schedule for the next day. Or hope the phone will ring."*
8. *"I'd rather eat."*

Ordinarily, a husband's sexual idiosyncrasies simply compound the tedium. Although technically the problems are his, she gets to be the scapegoat. Nora's exotic experience is a sample:

> *For years he called me "a lousy lay" when actually he was the one with the beautiful hang-ups. For example, he couldn't come. For hours he would go on and on without enjoyment until he got crazy. But he didn't want to give up. He insisted I should stuff things up his ass. I'd never known a man like him and I felt repulsed and contemptuous.*

More typical is the waiting situation described by Denise:

> *When my husband worked the evening shift, I had to wait until 11 p.m. to eat. By that time I was starving to death. It was the same thing with sex: We had it when he wanted it. His rules were that I couldn't grab him or aggressively initiate sex. I had to seduce him, either by my manner or clothing. It was waiting, waiting, and I couldn't stand that.*
>
> *By the time we'd been married five years, I considered his body a mine field, not during sex but before. I was never sure if I was touching the wrong place. I got very edgy and our sexual relationship totally deteriorated.*

If boredom doesn't undercut a woman's sex life, political warfare does. Her resentments simmer just short of the explosion point. But since she can't express them directly and since he's not listening anyway when she unleashes a watered- down blast of fury, she takes revenge by directing nuclear warheads at his most vulnerable spot. His genitals.

Expressing hostility by withdrawal from sex is so common that even men have noticed it. Marriage experts who cluck disapprovingly at such naughtiness usually spout fatherly homilies like, "Sex withholding is not only a cruel but an unrewarding ploy." This shows what they know. Cruel yes, unrewarding no. Because they make several assumptions which may be unwarranted:

1. That the woman was erotically interested in the man when she married him.
2. That her husband satisfies her in bed.
3. That moments still remain when she feels genuine affection for him. The more resentments she accumulates, however, the rarer these moments become. What men don't seem to understand is that, unlike themselves, women have trouble screwing people they don't like.

The reward of withholding sex is sublimely simple: She avoids sleeping with a person she doesn't particularly want in the first place. The situation calls for a premarital game, Thank You for a Lovely Evening, but seeing as how sex is now one of her primary wifely duties, the idea must be regretfully discarded. Her search for methods of passive resistance may be limited to wishful thinking. Edith tries to dispose of sex as quickly as possible:

> *My prayer is that my husband should develop a premature ejaculation problem. When I first found out what premature ejaculation meant, I*

> *thought to myself, "How great! Where do I find a man like that?"*
>
> *I would make some premature ejaculator very happy.*

In time, a woman grasps the problem and comes up with a workable solution: Too Tired Tonight. This technique for avoiding a sexual confrontation demands a certain amount of skull practice. Deborah outlines the preparation:

> *One of the games I first played was to develop a headache right after dinner. Then I moved up the time to the minute he came home from work. The trouble was, I never knew if I were hitting the mark because sometimes he didn't seem to catch on that a headache meant no sex. Since I don't need him to tell me to take a couple of aspirin, I rarely bother with that game anymore.*
>
> *Now I call him up at work and complain I'm having a rotten day. But more and more, I'm stopping the games; I just say, "I'm not in the mood." Or, "I'm too tired." The real solution would be separate bedrooms.*

When Too Tired Tonight is not strategically indicated, the alternative is to climb in next to her spouse and play the wife's much-touted bedtime game, Orgasm. Enacted by an experienced wife, it goes like this:

> *Husband: "Did you come?"*
> *Wife: "Of course, dear."*

Once she's said, "Of course," the man assumes he is performing satisfactorily and eventually stops asking altogether or only inquires routinely. For a change of pace, she can garnish the dialogue to prove she's having fun, too.

Husband: "Did you come?"
Wife: "No, dear, but don't worry. I love being close to you."

A logical question would be *why* she has to fake at all. April provides a perspective:

> *I remember hearing a bunch of women talking about what really turns them on. One claimed it was the feel of a man's back. "It better turn you on," I said, "because feeling his back is about all we ever get to do."*
>
> *That is, if a woman's lucky and he hasn't pinned her hands down to the bed. If I ask George to turn on his side, he says he can't come that way. If I ask him to get on the bottom, he's incredibly offended. "Move your hand," I say. No, he just can't make it that way. So he doesn't move his hand.*
>
> *But I'm supposed to lie spread-eagled on the bed and enjoy 180 pounds banging away at my crotch. And have an orgasm while I'm at it.*
>
> *No wonder women scratch when they fake passion. It's because they're being suffocated.*

Faking rapture from flat on her back is a technique generally mastered overnight. Performance needn't be perfect because the audience is never critical about delivery. They just want to hear the words clearly. Even though most women show a flair for Orgasm from the outset, the novice can make mistakes:

Husband: "Did you come?"
Diplomatic Wife: "You mean it's over?"

Husband: "Did you come?"
Semi-Bitchy Wife: "Of course not, klutz. I haven't begun.

> *Husband: "Did you come?"*
> *Bitchy Wife: "Whatsamatter, Orville? You impotent or something?"*

Amateur responses of this type deflate a husband's ego, not to mention his penis. Even if she hasn't read it in the *Ladies' Home Journal,* she finds it out soon enough for herself. On the other hand, the *Journal's* guidelines seem to be far from reliable when they suggest she might tell the truth. As it's unlikely she survived virginity and single life without being called a frigid bitch by some meatball she didn't want to bed down with, she's not about to leave herself open to name-calling now that she's married.

To squelch a nasty male rumor, wives rarely brood about faking orgasms. Felicia shrugs it off philosophically:

> *I'm a terrific panter. When Morris asks, I pant like crazy and say, "Yes, yes, you were wonderful." He believes he has only to put it in, ejaculate, and I have an orgasm automatically.*
>
> *He'd be shattered if I told him. Besides, it wouldn't do any good. Sex puts him to sleep and in a few minutes he's snoring.*

April's faking takes male fantasies into consideration:

> *One afternoon when our kids were at school, Isabel and I snuck off to see the movie,* Tits. *There was this man in the film who really dug breasts. He liked to lick them. After sucking away for a while, he bragged how he'd even brought women to orgasm just by licking their breasts.*
>
> *Well, when I heard that, I couldn't help howling out loud. I whooped, "HAH, HA!" I said to Isabel, "It must have taken the bastard forty-eight hours to do it." At which point, the guy went on to admit that* sometimes *it takes him a while.* Sometimes?
>
> *Do you suppose those poor women being licked*

> *by that idiot were actually expected to have real orgasms? Finally they had to fake it. I mean, after a while you shit or get off the pot.*

How to Drive a Husband to Infidelity Without His Ever Suspecting. A person can get fed up with Orgasm and Too Tired Tonight. Every so often, when she needs a complete cessation of sexual hostilities, she strikes.

Suppose, for instance, her husband were to fill his sexual needs elsewhere? What if she were to give him a helpful nudge? From this promising beginning, she builds up to one of women's greatest daredevil games, How to Drive a Husband to Infidelity Without His Ever Suspecting. Like straightforward talk with men on most subjects, the outright suggestion of infidelity rarely works. Natalie tried it:

> *I told him to look elsewhere. "Find someone," I said. "You'd enjoy sex more than with me." He travels a lot. He's good looking.*
>
> *He looked at me in amazement. Finally he claimed that the opportunity had never presented itself.*

Deborah made a tentative start by condoning *Playboy* magazine:

> *He has his* Playboys *in the basement, ten years of back issues. He won't throw them out because he's paid for them and anything he pays for, he doesn't throw away. Actually, he doesn't read them; he just looks at the pictures. Once he remarked that if I were more affectionate, he wouldn't need* Playboy. *Well, I know I can function as a sexual being because I've had good sex with other men, so it's not* my *problem. "That's the way I am," I answered. "I'm just not an outgoing, affectionate*

> *person. If it turns you on to look at breasts, good. Read your* Playboys *then. It doesn't bother me."*
>
> *But, to be honest, I do think he's a little immature.*

Deborah then moved into Stage Two of her campaign with a sex schedule which is suitable for framing:

> *For years he drove me crazy about sex. The arguments always ended with me apologizing. When he thought we weren't doing it often enough, he'd make nasty, hurtful remarks to the effect that I was frigid. I concluded it was easier to do it and get it out of the way. So I suggested a schedule. "Don't bug me on Wednesday," I said, "because that's my club night. Don't bug me on Saturday night because we're entertaining or going out. Don't bug me around the kids." And so on. "But—we can have sex Sunday nights and I promise to put forth my best effort." I'm usually pretty relaxed on Sundays.*
>
> *He vetoed the idea: "I can't have sex on a schedule." He didn't feel it would be spontaneous.*
>
> *But we tried it anyway and the schedule has worked out okay. It's not a big production like he feared and I can mentally prepare myself.*
>
> *Every once in a while he still grumbles that I'm doing it as a duty but I ignore him.*

Although a wife pins her hopes on his eventually finding an obliging secretary with a heart of gold, she refrains from asking questions. If her marital sex life begins to drop off encouragingly, she has her answer.

According to sexual statisticians, infidelity among married men has risen to an all-time high of seventy-five percent. Furthermore, they say, only twenty-five percent of the wives confronted with an unfaithful husband sue for divorce. Which seems reasonable enough.

The Double Standard Revisited. Inspiring a husband to adultery solves half the problem. Before a woman goes entirely to seed, there's her own sex life to worry about. At one time or another, usually on those days when she's sorry she's not single again, she examines the possibility of bootleg sex.

However, when it comes right down to actually doing something about it, many wives feel reluctant. The reasons are practical rather than moral. What with the kids hanging around, an affair appears to invite troubles she doesn't need. More important, she normally has contact with an undesirable group of men: the husbands of her friends. She has heard about their sexual inadequacies so frequently that sleeping with one of them holds small temptation. Deborah writes off the idea immediately:

> *I could jump into bed with Randall but I'm not that dopey. When I'm visiting Joan and him for dinner, he waits until she's busy in the kitchen and then pulls me down on his lap. I just get back up and forget it. I don't have any respect for him but he's a nice enough person.*
>
> *Now, Donna's husband is a sneak. He never showed any interest in me as an intelligent human being and then one morning he called up to invite me over for coffee. Naturally I assumed Donna would be there but I find she's out for the day and there he is in his underpants. I told him to have the decency to get dressed. Damn right I told Donna. She ought to know what he's up to.*

In Natalie's case, however, she slept with the husband of her best friend, Rosemary, precisely because she knew he was still virile:

> *At this point in my life, all the men I meet are someone's husband. I prefer to have an extramarital thing with a family man simply because it's the*

> *safest type of relationship for me. I'm not hunting for another husband, so I don't want to get emotionally involved. Nor do I want what happens more often, to have a man get emotionally involved with me.*
>
> *Rosemary had been telling me for years how good Johnny was in bed. Now, I wouldn't screw up a friend's marriage but at that time she was having an affair with a hippie she'd met at a rock festival and I knew she'd appreciate someone distracting Johnny. She was happy to shove him out the door and aim him at my house. I don't think he ever suspected.*
>
> *He was a good sex partner, but he bored me after a while because all he ever wanted to talk about were his problems with Rosemary. I'd heard them from her and now I had to listen to his side of the story. I didn't bother to hide my boredom because if, God forbid, I'd showed too much interest, I never would have got rid of him. He couldn't accept the fact that my sole interest in him was sexual. I wasn't interested in hearing about his money problems and, even if I had, I sure wasn't going to give him the $39 in my secret bank account.*

Jealous husbands are mostly in the movies. In real life, they rarely believe their loyal wives capable of such guile. Knee-deep in neighborly sexual intrigue, Natalie wonders at her husband's lack of perception:

> *What I can't understand is that he knows I'm capable of great deviousness, that I had a sordid past with men before we were married, and yet he didn't confront me with any suspicions. I suppose he wants to trust me. In his eyes, I'm pure because that's the kind of wife he wants. Take the business about Johnny and the rubbers.*
>
> *My husband had a vasectomy, which solved his*

birth control problem but not mine. So when he was away on a business trip and I was planning in advance to sleep with Johnny, I remembered some leftover rubbers upstairs in his drawer and brought them down for Johnny to use. I was going to ask Johnny to replace them but I didn't get a chance because my husband came back early.

I thought it out from every possible angle and decided to mess up the drawer and blame it on one of the kids. I scribbled on some papers with crayon, dropped one of the rubbers on the floor, and flushed the rest down the toilet. When he got home, I didn't say, "Oh, do you know what Peter did today?" I just let him discover the mess for himself.

Gloria believes that the nuisance of conducting an extramarital affair is a small price to pay. Before she married, she'd been sleeping with two men:

Very soon after Ray and I married, maybe less than three months, I resumed my affair with Tommy. I never would have married him but he was super in bed. I didn't see why I should give up good sex just because I was married.

After several years of hearing how she was, in her husband's opinion anyway, "a cold cunt," Yvette wanted to investigate the truth of the charge:

I began to feel abnormal because I didn't want sex as often as he did. Then I had a relationship with someone else and found out my sex drive wasn't as low as my husband claimed. But while the affair was good for my morale, I think the main reason I got involved was boredom. It turned out to be a stopgap because as soon as I got a job, I entirely lost interest in the man. As far as I'm concerned,

> *sex is something to do when there's nothing better to do. Even when I'm attracted to the man.*

Denise, now divorced, regrets the wasted years:

> *When I was married, I never slept with anyone else. I made a big production out of being a faithful wife. I had to be screwy because now I realize that I could have slept with another man and still had exactly the same miserable relationship with Barney. I think I must have been crazy.*

VI. BABY GAMES

Glorious Motherhood. Any misgivings Little Darling once may have had about marriage appeared insignificant when compared with the alternative: the various humiliations of being an "old maid." Still, she hadn't envisioned marriage to be quite the drag it turned out. For one thing, the prospects look bleak for ever achieving her master plan, coexistence with The Breadwinner. However, all is not in vain, for, hallelujah, there's one game she has reserved for use at a strategic moment. She introduces Glorious Motherhood.

Although she can see that motherhood has striking disadvantages, taking care of children for one, nonetheless, it appears to be a solution. Since her husband seldom talks to her unless he's delivering an oration or distributing instructions, she feels isolated. Not only would a child provide company, but it also might lift the domestic tension. On the one hand, what does she need with more children when she already has one? On the other hand, there's this empty womb standing around doing nothing. After weighing the pros and cons, she astounds her husband by her overnight transformation into a nymphomaniac and succeeds in getting herself pregnant in record time. Then, like Denise, she may regret it immediately:

I deliberately became pregnant for a combination of reasons. I knew my husband would approve and I also wanted to be recognized in the world. But there was something else, too. It was obvious that my husband didn't appreciate my presence. Oh, he wanted me around but I shouldn't ask for his attention or impose myself on him. Since I'm over five feet tall, I could contain myself only so much. I thought a child would at least mean another person in the house.

When I got pregnant, he was thrilled and I felt miserable. I knew I didn't really want a baby. I said to myself, "Don't kid yourself about this. You should get an abortion." At which point Barney pulled a superb strategy: He calmly withdrew. "Do what you want," he said, "Don't let me influence you." He continued to talk but he suddenly wasn't accessible anymore. At the same time, I had no idea of how to go about finding an abortionist. So I had the baby.

After the baby was born and I was going completely bananas to the extent that I wanted to give the child away, I learned that my husband was going to fix up a friend with the name of an abortionist. The whole time he'd had an abortionist in his back pocket. I wanted to kill him.

But, you see, I've always been inadequate. If I had been adequate, I would have done anything to find an abortionist. I would have called up every woman I'd ever met. I would have stood on the Empire State Building and shouted for one.

Glorious Motherhood milks one of man's all-time great mottos: Treat a pregnant woman with tender loving care. For nine months then, a woman can be fairly certain of getting her husband's help around the house. He will vacuum the rugs and occasionally cook. There are limits, however. Not even for a pregnant woman will he clean the oven.

Since ample discomforts accompany pregnancy, the extra

weight if nothing else, a wife can exploit her condition as she chooses. Possibly best of all, she has a ready-made excuse from sex for six weeks or more. For that reason alone, pregnancy can be worth it.

Another encouraging development is that, at long last, her husband has become solicitous, attentive, and perhaps even talkative. The transformation will be temporary, however, because once her belly subsides, he returns to his former self, frozen and self-absorbed. Meanwhile, displaying her stomach as proof of his manhood, the expectant Daddy proudly shows off his wife. As far as she can tell, his part in the whole affair was minimal, but she plays Keeping One's Mouth Shut. April examines the role of the sperm:

> *When men talk about conception, there's always the allusion to the "seed" and how it is spilled into a woman. I get the picture of the sperm swimming vigorously about in the vaginal canal while the big, lazy egg lolls around waiting or slowly drifts down to meet it. Then there's a blare of trumpets as Supersperm bombards the egg.*
>
> *Presto, it's the miracle of life, brought about by—ta,ta—Supersperm. It would make a great comic strip.*

The expectant Daddy's delight is predicated on his belief that he won't have to look after the child. Too lazy to attend to his own personal upkeep, he shudders at the idea of caring for another's. If he suspected there were the remotest chance that child care would be his responsibility, he'd drag his wife to an abortionist in the ninth month.

And then there are the men who exhibit skittishness about fatherhood no matter what. Although Amanda's husband insisted he wanted a child, during most of her pregnancy he couldn't be located:

> *The realization that I was pregnant made me extremely upset. Two things stopped me from*

> *having an abortion: I didn't know where to find an abortionist and my husband objected. In fact, he made me feel so guilty that I gave up the idea. Once I decided to have the baby, however, he began to freak out. Even though he knew I was upset about pregnancy, he suddenly began spending most of his time away from home. Although he came in to sleep, usually he was off visiting friends or working at his studio. Often I didn't know where he was.*
>
> *Before the pregnancy, I suspected he didn't care about me. I took his absence as proof.*

Before long, Glorious Motherhood benches the expectant Daddy. The person replacing him is the obstetrician, a man who has a hard time remembering a woman's name from one month to the next. Aside from waiters, obstetricians rate as the world's foremost male chauvinist pigs. On the first appointment to confirm her pregnancy, the doctor extorts a $10 lab fee for a rabbit test because he can't tell if she's pregnant. She knows; she hasn't been fornicating madly for nothing. On the second visit, he addresses her by her first name, but reciprocal privileges are not forthcoming.

By the third month, when she's burning to know what horrors await her, he treats her like a troublesome child in the Why? stage. Her questions are answered by soothing admonitions not to worry and to leave everything to him. Since he can't remember her name—first or last—she finds this a disturbing idea. Still ignorant, however, she has little choice but to place her wavering faith in him.

By the end of nine months, at precisely the time when she most needs confidence, dignity, and maturity to cope with childbirth and a newborn infant, he has succeeded in reducing her to the state of a three-year-old. Knowing little or nothing about the realities of childbirth, not from the obstetrician anyway, she enters labor full of ignorance, terror, and prayers that he will anesthetize her as quickly as possible. Childbirth is one stage of Glorious Motherhood she'd prefer to skip. Three ungrateful patients recall their obstetricians:

> ROBERTA - *Obstetricians are in a classic position of male authority which I despise. I had a team of good- looking OB's who were in their thirties. I found it impossible to actually criticize them to their faces for withholding information or giving me unsatisfactory answers. After I left their office, I'd be in a rage. But if a woman stands up and protests, she's a bitch, right? I didn't want to be a bitch.*

> GLORIA - *He regarded his patients as children. To get any information, I had to ask over and over. He never volunteered anything. His attitude seemed to be that what I didn't know wouldn't hurt me.*
>
> *He'd flash into the examining room, check my folder to see who I was, and go into his everything's-okay-little-girl spiel. I didn't want reassurance; I wanted facts. Didn't I have to do anything to give birth? Not according to him. Just present my body like a side of beef and he'd do the rest. He thought he was God.*
>
> *When I told him I planned to have natural childbirth, he sulked for three months. Apparently he regarded a patient who was awake during labor and delivery as a gross inconvenience. It would take some of the glory away from him. He didn't understand why a woman wanted to be awake at the birth and, heavens, push out her own baby. "Well, if you really want to," he said, as if I had asked to witness a hanging.*
>
> *During labor, he'd run in periodically to push his Demerol. He was in an obvious snit because I refused it and yet wasn't writhing in pain.*
>
> *Afterward he came into the recovery room, still*

miffed, and said, "Next time, why don't you stay home and deliver the baby yourself?"

I thought to myself, "Righto, you bastard."

YVETTE - After I had a miscarriage, my doctor performed a D and C. Later, when he came to unpack the gauze, he needed something to put under me. He must have felt too goddammed lazy to call for a nurse because he saw my newspaper lying on a chair next to the bed and shoved it under me. He managed to turn a mildly embarrassing but common medical procedure into an unforgettably degrading experience. He behaved as though he were cleaning up after a dog.

This man is now chief of ob-gyn at ___ Hospital.

The Case of the Missing Daddy. The Little Darling who once puzzled over her Daddy's whereabouts gradually begins to accept her own husband's role as absentee seigneur. In a way, she's relieved, for motherhood has reinforced her power position. Although the contest isn't over yet, numerically, at least, she's ahead. While the kids still may be unable to distinguish one team from the other, they know who's in charge of their lives.

But for all the political advantages of motherhood, a woman quickly understands she may have made a whacking strategic error by locking the main gate of the labor camp and tossing away the key. By and by, she discovers the secret Daddy sensed all along: Round-the-clock child care is no fun. Admission that she's been bamboozled is taboo. It seems like every time she picks up a magazine, she spots a stern reminder from some man who's yet to change a diaper: "It is a rare and exceptionally gifted woman who does something more important in the outside world than she does during those critical first six years when she is helping to form the personality and character of a child."

"Rare and exceptionally gifted" is certainly not a

description she would ever apply to herself. On the other hand, if the idea were true, then why don't men stay home those critical first six years? In any case, she keeps her opinions to herself or shares them with folks in the same boat. Aside from mothering and housekeeping, her chief activity is chatting with other frazzled mothers. Predictably, their favorite subject is themselves.

As frustrating as a woman's verbal encounters with her husband have been so far, now she rarely shares her uppermost thoughts: toilet training, shoe tying, the concept of sharing, keeping the kids out of the refrigerator, and why does her daughter hate her so? Daddy, only too relieved at his narrow escape from child duty, has more important matters on his mind than who hit who at the sandbox today. He's too busy putting a man on the moon and inventing electric tie racks.

On this plateau of desperation, then, she opens Phase Two of Glorious Motherhood, a half-hearted attempt to wheedle Daddy's help with the children. This idea, she knows in advance, will be futile but since one of her favorite fantasies is Daddy stranded on a desert island with a dozen diaper-wetting toddlers, she gives it a try. Daddies are hardly notorious for baby-sitting, and her husband turns out to be no exception. One version or another of the fantasy, however, lives on. Amanda thinks longingly:

> *If there were any capable male baby-sitters, I'd hire one.*
> *Why?*
> *To make a man suffer the way I have.*

In Phase Three, she brings forward a radical proposition for negotiation:

> *Glorious Mother: "Maybe I should go back to work. We need the money."*
> *Daddy: "But who will look after the kids?"*
> *Glorious Mother "Well, there are day care centers, you know."*

Daddy: "Day care! My child in an institution! Never!"

As Daddy well knows, he already has a free day care center for his children, a one-woman establishment called Mother.

Reading everything she can find on the boons of preschool education, she holds on impatiently for another year or two until she can cajole Daddy into financing a more acceptable version of day care, nursery school. Regretfully, nursery school sessions run only half a day which hardly leaves time for a decent orgy at the A & P. But she's too grateful to carp about details. If anyone asks her to name the best moment of her day, she unthinkingly blurts out the truth: After the kids are in bed.

Something has gone wrong. She suffers from a mysterious malaise which introspection reveals to be part physical, part spiritual. Tackling the problem from the outside in, she notes that her body is describably dreadful: she weighs fifteen pounds more than she did when she married which is hardly surprising because one of her few pleasures these days is eating. If she can convince her doctor that she needs "something to curb my appetite just a little," maybe she can walk away with a prescription for Eskatrol and get on with the next stage in her life. Pill-popping is the biggest thing to happen to her since she discovered the lascivious potential of the A & P.

Because she's never been depressed a day in her life, or so she tells herself, she refuses to recognize her condition for what it is. In any event, she's overjoyed to know that someone, if only the pharmaceutical industry, is thinking of her. Slowly she goes about stocking an arsenal of mother's helpers, prescriptions for Librium, Elavil, Equanil, Tofranil, Seconal, Nembutal, and other precious potions. If her doctor is the balky type, she's not above coaxing a sympathetic sandbox mother into sharing her prescription.

Usually the pills are hidden and rationed out for emergencies. If the emergencies begin to occur daily, she may be forced to play Glorious Motherhood to its final, surrealistic round. This means a major policy statement to the effect that she's become unglued. It takes such an announcement because Daddy hadn't really noticed for himself although now he may be shocked into paying for some kind of treatment. Here she's on fairly safe ground because the male establishment accepts neurosis in women as a perfectly normal condition. It must, male researchers solemnly hypothesize, be related to hormones and premenstrual blues. Should Daddy object, a soul-buddy like this Yale University psychiatrist will be happy to set him straight: "The family should be sympathetic, supporting, and understanding. They should realize that it's just not normal for a mother to go on for a long time being tearful and bitchy and not getting her housework done."

As far as Daddy can observe, tears and bitchiness have been part of his wife's normal behavior for years. He can continue to live with them. But the possibility of her failing to do the housework is serious. He pays.

Sooner or later, a wife is forced to deal with basic issues. She asks herself:

> *Can I endure living in the uninhabitable institution of marriage?*
> *Or, can I endure the man I married?*
> *Or, can I anesthetize myself sufficiently with the help of Librium, brandy alexanders, and cable television?*

In the end, these explorations are beside the point. The $64 question is: Who will take care of me?

Since it's the unique wife who can answer "I will," she goes on slugging it out with the Head of the Household until such time as they arrive at a nonaggression treaty. But if the odds for survival appear overwhelmingly against her, Little Darling secretly makes plans to withdraw and fight again another day.

SIX

Truth and Consequences

I. BREAKUP GAMES
- Leveling At Last
- Eleventh Hour Rescue
- Move

II. LEGAL GAMES
- Our Money
- Our Children
- Male Chauvinist Pig Attorneys

III. THERAPY GAMES
- Character Assassination
- Nora's Diary
- Reflections on One's Future

Truth and Consequences

If there's one time a man might feel confident of getting real insights into a woman, it's during separation and divorce. At last it looks like the hot war. But hold on ...

Undoubtedly, divorce is a wife's bank holiday. For a change of pace, she can forget her usual workaday games and luxuriate in the rare pleasure of a dirty fight. Best of all, divorce ends in her reprieve from institutional living. No longer is she obligated to live a husband's life to the fullest, handhold his ego, and get up at 6:45 (when he does) so that she'll be ready to go to bed at 10 (when he does). It's farewell to moving when he gets a promotion, so long to courses in Creative Macrame (Wednesdays 7:00-9:00 p.m.) because a wife should develop outside interests.

Still, she doesn't allow freedom to fog her judgment. While a good many of her hostilities are finally out in the open, she has enough sense to know that total honesty will backfire. One of the main things she has to lose is money.

Consider this chapter as simply another stanza of womankind's theme song: Survival

I. BREAKUP GAMES

Leveling At Last. Among the Libriums and other fairy tale elixirs Little Darling so heedlessly swallows is the bitter pill of truth: Cinderella and the prince do not necessarily live happily ever after. The omens were there all the time had she wished to recognize them. Looking back, she can see that the prince was a jerk anyway. Even so, the fairy tales which enchanted her so many decades ago are not easily abandoned. Unfortunately, their picture of a woman's destiny established her expectations about marriage. All she had to do was wait until a rescuing, protective male rode up. Never again would she have to concern herself about such cruelties of life as the need for grocery money. Living happily ever after with the prince—*one* prince—meant a swell lifetime deal. No mention was made of princesses who blew it. Apparently none did.

A woman doesn't write off her dreams overnight. As Judy explains, it's usually a long, tortuous, secretive process:

> *After I'd been married about two years, maybe sooner, I knew that eventually I would leave him. The idea was so scary that I didn't think about it often but I couldn't see myself spending my entire life with him.*
>
> *The only question was "When?" Eight years and two children later I knew the time had come. My husband said I was selfish to break up our marriage so casually. "You should never have had children," he told me. "It's not fair to them."*
>
> *I didn't tell him that my decision certainly wasn't casual. Nor that I deliberately waited until I'd had children.*

A strategy for retreat must be carefully mapped out in advance. Her reconnaissance begins by consulting former wives for information on what it's like out in the cold world without a make-believe prince. Even with her married friends, she blabs incessantly as she investigates the routes to freedom. At the sandbox within earshot of her children, in the checkout line at the Super Giant, at parties to which she experimentally goes alone now, she schemes out loud to any woman who will listen. There's no need to caution, "Don't tell my husband." Nor is there danger of the kids squealing.

While she broadcasts her plans to many people, her husband is not among them. In fact, any clues dropped by mistake aren't picked up. Denise remembers the last anniversary:

> *For a long time I knew I was going to leave him. I'd admitted this to myself and discussed it a bit with others.*
>
> *To my husband, I only hinted. As our arguments escalated and it became embarrassing to be around other people, I thought my feelings must be obvious. On our last wedding anniversary, friends came over for champagne. All evening I was really putting down the whole anniversary scene; indirectly I tried to tell Barney. I just never expressed it to his face.*
>
> *My leaving depended on one question: Would I have enough money? I was earning $125 a week which I knew wouldn't make it. But I had an opportunity for a job paying more, a job which would change my life because for the first time I would be free to think of leaving my husband and child. I knew that I was going to leave the child with Barney.*
>
> *But the job wasn't certain.*

However useful the tactical advantage of a surprise attack might be, this is not what motivates her secrecy. Rather, it's uncertainty that she can pull off the stunt because, in the end, withdrawal depends entirely on economics. The *little* woman who supposedly has trouble balancing her checking account now embarks on a complex series of calculations which would awe a CPA. She begins by searching for their most recent income tax return, a document which has never interested her before. Once she has established the exact amount of *our* money, her reckoning may run like this: The Breadwinner earns, let's say, $15,000. Surely he won't mind parting with a paltry $100 a week. Okay, that's $5,200 right there but clearly not enough to support herself and three children. Okay, she will find a job, one that pays $10,000. You bet. Now she has $15,200 and the beginning of hope. By the end, when she has become an expert on the economics of divorce, she will find out:

1. The Breadwinner is a stingy bastard.
2. Even if she wrings a crummy $5,200 out of him, she must pay taxes on some or all of the money.
3. No employer considers her worth $10,000 a year. She's lucky to get a part-time secretarial job paying $65 a week (before taxes).

Our money plus her salary add up to a gross of only $8,580. But by the time she finds this out, it's too late to turn back. Nor would she if she could.

In addition to her computations, she's equally busy performing cosmetic surgery on her self-image which has been, and still is, that of a klutz. The area most desperately in need of the knife is her guts, which happened to be the subject of Leah's pep talks:

> *The idea of actually leaving him scared me. I told myself over and over, "This is going to take guts." Somewhere, buried down deep, I thought I must have guts.*

Approaching the point of no return, Libby found it helpful to look in the mirror as she delivered a stern lecture:

> *One night I looked at myself in the bathroom mirror. "What gives with you?" I asked. "You're twenty-seven. You don't need this."*
>
> *During the day I worked; in the evening, he expected me to wait on him and cook gourmet meals. Because I was tired, I stopped taking care of myself. Not only did I feel depressed but I also looked a horror. He made me feel like such a worthless piece of shit that I didn't care what happened to me.*

After a lifetime of waiting—waiting for the prince, waiting for the prince to show up for dinner—a woman can wait a little longer. She's in no hurry to break the news to her husband. Small incidents such as the one chronicled by Leah may edge her closer to the brink, but still she remains silent:

> *All of my family had gathered at my sister's house for her birthday party. Harry was talking about the war and, for the millionth time, describing the rats. When I tried to break into his monologue, he snarled. "Who do you think you're interrupting? Shut your goddammed mouth."*
>
> *That did it. I left him a week later.*

Finally—D day. Leah chose an appropriate stage for her announcement:

> *I turned to him in bed and said, "I'm leaving." He grabbed my arm and began to twist. "Brother," I told him, "you just killed what little respect I had for you and it wasn't much. Now take your paws off me." When he didn't let go, I started to kick him.*
>
> *While I was packing, he cried, "Let's try and work it out. I'll go to a psychiatrist." Once before I had suggested a psychiatrist because I felt he was mentally unbalanced.*

And now does a woman level with a man? Does she give him so much as a capsule summary of what it's been like as his wife? No. Three wives found themselves tongue-tied:

> *AMANDA - At the end I didn't show him how angry I actually felt. I said nothing because there was nothing to say. The emotional turmoil of constant fighting had left me exhausted. I waited until I couldn't take anymore and then simply left.*
>
> *Come to think of it, I didn't tell him I was leaving. I said, "I'm going home for Christmas." He didn't comment when I packed my largest suitcase.*

NORA - Telling him was too big an effort. It would have taken too long and, at that point, I had more important matters on my mind. He wanted to analyze what went wrong; I wanted him to move out. If I'd started a commotion, I felt he'd never go. I suppose I let him believe there was hope for a reconciliation. I knew perfectly well I never wanted to live with him again but I was too tired for scenes. I didn't exactly lie to him, but I wasn't truthful either.

The month after he moved out was the happiest I'd had in years. I didn't want to spoil it by seeing or talking to him. Getting rid of him gave me a tremendous sense of well-being which didn't wear off until I hit the problems of being on my own with a small child.

LIBBY - Even after the divorce I didn't tell him how I really felt. I never said, "You treated me like shit. The years I lived with you were a humiliation."

I was a jerk to have hidden my contempt but I still had a great fear of him which was hard to explain to people. I remember a friend asking me, "What are you afraid of?" Maybe it was an overreaction but I was petrified. It went guts deep.

Eleventh-Hour Rescues. Seldom does a husband accept the breakup of his marriage with the dispassion for which his sex is famous. In most cases, his initial reaction is stupefaction. He may loathe his wife. He may have itched to give *her* the sack. Within a week, he'll be in some other woman's bed, if he isn't there already. But he panics anyway because a man reluctantly gives up property he's bought and paid for.

He had good reason to feel upset. The domestic help situation being what it is today, he's aware that maids are expensive. What a comedown it would be to shop, cook, clean, and rinse out his own jockey shorts. There's a further pulverizing thought. Suppose he must care for the children? And finally he remembers to clutch his wallet. (It's still there, but not for long.) After all those forgettable years of free service, the hot and cold running meals, the millions of clean socks, after all that, is it possible that he might have to pay her for *not* taking his suits to the cleaners? The idea is too fantastic, not to mention unjust, to be credible.

More unmanning, however, is her brass to suggest that she can do without him. Apparently she has forgotten that she can't support herself, can't keep her bank account straight, can't open mayonnaise jars, and, my God, can't even handle the children without calling him at the office to report they're driving her barmy, can't manage alone for a week when he goes on a business trip, can't stop harping about loneliness. It must, he decides, be an early menopause. Or she's just having her period. And besides, she hasn't given him one good reason for wanting to split up.

As a result of her husband's disbelief, a wife always gets a chance to repent. It leaves room for a crackerjack parting game, Can This Marriage Be Saved? which lends much-needed comic relief to what would otherwise be a dreary grace period. At this point, a wife has nothing to lose by humoring her spouse. Is it possible that this shock is just what he needs to become a decent husband? Frankly, she doubts it, but you never know. Her main reason for lingering, however, is guilt. A soon-to-be-dumped Daddy invariably thinks of the children. His standard charge is that only a monster could separate a man from his offspring. Most likely his wife feels like Leah:

> *Jason was only fourteen months old. Did I have the right to deprive him of his father? This bothered me for awhile. Then I asked myself, "Is Harry much of a father to begin with?" The answer was "No."*

But for decency's sake, she feels obliged to offer a reasonable facsimile of remorse whether she feels it or not.

As a result, she soon finds herself in the office of a person responsible for oiling and repairing the institutions which keep a man's world going. The counseling sessions with the marriage expert, the psychiatrist, or the psychologist provide extra inning highlights of Can This Marriage Be Saved? A wife may walk off the field crying or laughing, but in either case she has confirmed what she always suspected. Denise merely felt depressed:

> *Our marriage had grown so hideous that Barney said, "We gotta do something."*
>
> *I said, "There are three alternatives. One is for us to break up, two is to go to a therapist, and ..."*
>
> *I don't remember the third. Anyway, he chose the therapist. The four sessions were quite a revelation. I remember my husband saying, "All I ever asked her to do was wake me in the morning and make my dinner." That was what he wanted out of marriage. An alarm clock and a cook. Nothing else. Not companionship or love or sex.*

Nora was able to exit without remorse:

> *When the marriage counselor asked him if he thought the marriage was worth saving, he said, "Yes, Nora is a darn good cook. She's better than my mother." I wanted to howl hysterically. His mother! If he could have fucked his mother, he wouldn't have married.*

Ordinarily a wife must endure one more last-ditch attempt to stall her departure. Recalling the traditional male prescription for an uppity woman, her husband invariably tries to maneuver her into bed. This seems like a logical solution because, even though she has scorned him sexually for years, this may be precisely her trouble. She doesn't get enough. At any rate, sexual activity often resumes for a brief period. Denise reports on the final bouts in conjugal passion:

We were visiting my mother when something unusual happened: He put his head on my lap. I started to play with his hair and soon he was grooving and I was grooving. I felt two things. One was a warm, wonderful melting sensation and the other an urge to pummel him to death. I wanted to scream, "Why did you deprive me of this for all those years?"

Then, we went on a vacation shortly before we separated. There was more opportunity for sex than at home, and I asked him to play with my clitoris. I began having wonderful orgasms. After a week or so, he got impatient: "I'm not going to do this all the time, you know."

"All right," I thought, "I can do this to myself." I bought a vibrator. I would masturbate with the vibrator in front of him.

I think it was the vibrator which made him realize he'd have to let me go. The situation was too heavy. He couldn't deal with me anymore.

Reject, reject, reject. That's the way I ended my marriage. By my actions rather than words, I was telling him, "I won't cook for you anymore. I won't wait on you. And for sex, I'll use a vibrator."

Move. When a marriage breaks up, somebody has to leave. The law is unreasonably persnickety about granting separations or divorces to people still living at the same address. This presents a predicament because neither spouse may want to budge. Not surprisingly, the husband is usually the most reluctant. Not only is he accustomed to the baronial comforts of home, but moving entails inconveniences such as finding a place to move to, paying rent, and packing one hundred back issues of *Playboy*. Besides, what is a Head of Household without a household? Even if he appeared only occasionally to survey his property, he considers the homestead his. Not hers.

But the main reason a man hates to give up his cozy nest is service. True, the quality of restaurant service has slid downhill recently, but his wife still usually serves him dinner if he shows up to eat with the children. Laundry and maid service have also deteriorated badly, but they do function off and on. However poor the service has become, it beats the disastrous situation he'd face if he moved: namely, self-service. There's still another thought: If he doesn't move, his wife will have to give up her batty idea of separating.

Recognizing the odds against her husband moving voluntarily, a wife resolves to blast him loose from the premises if necessary. The name of her game: Move. Nora played it sweetly:

> *For months the atmosphere at home had been lethal. We didn't speak except to snarl. I couldn't understand why he wouldn't move. He always had some excuse. "I don't know where to go," he'd bawl. Or, "Andrea will be upset if I leave." Even though eventually I stopped cooking, moved into Andrea's room to sleep, never talked to him, even though it was obvious we couldn't stand each other, still he hung around.*
>
> *I reached the point where I would have done anything to get him out, even be nice to him. And that's exactly what I had to do. I suggested, "Why don't we live apart for awhile and see what happens? Then we'll be able to get a calmer perspective on our relationship."*
>
> *He reluctantly agreed and went to live with friends. He must have planned to return because he took only a few of his belongings. I felt sorry for him but I changed the lock on the door anyway.*

Come what may, a woman's determination to unload her husband isn't going to be thwarted by his refusal to leave. If necessary, the sentimental *little* woman, the one renowned in song and legend as the nestmaker, unhesitatingly packs up babies, dogs, gerbils, and one hundred back copies of *Cosmo* and leaves the honorable Head of Household to clean his own oven. Amanda moved, only to find her husband a few steps behind:

> *I left him twice and both times it was I who moved out. The first time, when Karin was ten months old, I found separation too difficult and I returned for nearly a year. But I knew all the while I would be going again once I could manage living on my own.*
>
> *One problem was the difficulty of getting an apartment. Landlords seem to be afraid that single women are hookers. Finally Daddy rented an apartment for me in his name. This turned out to be lucky for more than one reason. My husband wanted to reconcile and he tried to move in with me. I was able to say, "It's not my apartment, it's Daddy's. And he doesn't want you here."*

Denise's husband retained custody of their apartment and son:

> *When I first moved out, I had a hard time getting myself together. Although I was living with friends, I wanted my own place. I remember asking my husband for his advice which was, I should rent a room close by the apartment That's when I understood my husband's Rooming House Theory about my existence. He believed it was okay for me to live in a room, with the bath down the hall and cooking privileges, something I regard as half a life. He knows I'm young ... that I want to go out with other men ... that I want a whole life.*
>
> *Maybe he hoped we would reconcile. Maybe he thought I would be so miserable in a room that I'd come home. But I really think he wanted the convenience of having me close so that I could*

spend more time helping with the baby. Also a room would be cheap and, in the long run, that would mean more money for him. I got very angry.

If for no other reason, I wanted an apartment as a place to fuck in. Finally, when I did sublet a place, I put the mattress on the floor and bought pink sheets and an orange light. I prepared it specifically for the purpose of sex. My mother was dying to come over but I didn't let her.

II. LEGAL GAMES

Our Money. Even though Little Darling may conceal her true reasons for separating, divorce certainly provides a splendid opportunity to unmuzzle a few of her basic feelings. A woman suing for divorce can behave as bitchily as she likes without fear of social disapproval. Indeed, if she isn't a bitch, she can bank on serious trouble because, contrary to one of the myths men lovingly circulate, the "alimony racket" is rigged to benefit husbands. Ditto for the divorce laws. As a result, a wife has little chance of winning the legal games. The best she can hope for is to rack up as many points as possible.

Since her goal is financial survival, she introduces Alimony, a game requiring fancy footwork. Alimony gets off to a rousing start long before official legal proceedings begin; in most cases, the game opens with a light scrimmage when she attempts to reapportion *our* money, a move which her husband interprets as actively hostile. Of course, if she wants to be a first-class bitch, she cleans out their joint bank account, stocks up on six months' worth of groceries, and charges the children's school wardrobes *before* she announces her intention to split. It's a pity, but most wives lack this degree of foresight.

Starting with the premise that her years of faithful service as a live-in maid deserve recognition, she pursues what amounts to unemployment compensation and severance pay. She discovers that, as far as her husband is concerned, she rates nothing because nobody fired her. She quit. At the point where she decides friendly agreement is out of the question, she steers the game forward by calling in the law. By this time she's read half the books on how to get a divorce and is well on her way to becoming an expert. She knows, for example, that a husband is liable for support of his wife and children. Not fazed by her husband's attitude, she proceeds directly to a divorce attorney, not for a divorce but simply to make sure her husband coughs up the $100 a week she needs to survive. Shortly thereafter comes a cheering surprise which will sustain her during the ordeal ahead; namely, that divorcing her husband will hold many moments of vulgar pleasure. Nora savors the tip-off:

> *Getting the summons must have been a shock to him. Within minutes of the time he received it, he was on the phone to me. What did I mean by having it sent to his office? How outrageous! How crude! From his squeals of pain, you would have thought that I'd personally invented the entire judicial process.*
>
> *"Hot diggety dog," I thought. "If he's making a fuss over a little thing like the summons, just wait until he finds out what's ahead for him—alimony, child support, counsel fees."*
>
> *For the first time since I'd decided to divorce him, I began to feel good about it. I realized this was going to be fun.*

The first official jeers from the opposition camp, usually from the attorney hastily recruited to guard her husband's treasury, is an emphatic rejection of her demand for $100 a week temporary support. Thanks to her conscientious legal leg work, however, she will probably get the $100 or close to it, but her revels will be short-lived. Not only must she pay taxes, but $100 doesn't begin to cover her minimum expenses.

Fuel to sustain the legal battle comes from an unexpected

source: her husband. Over the female wire services flash late bulletins reporting that her estranged spouse has been cavorting all over town like a reincarnated playboy. She should have known. When he picks up the children, he mentions he hasn't eaten all day to save money—but she notices he's wearing a new suede jacket. According to him, her thievery and cupidity have reduced him to two martinis for lunch—but she sees the kids always returning with presents. Most infuriating, however, is the thought that he's spending *our* money on Joan and Carol and Sue and Alice and any other handy woman in his office. In Angela's case, this was the deciding factor which led her to demand alimony she hadn't wanted:

> *At the start I was a sap and felt sorry for him. I had a part-time job and I thought, "Well, I'll just ask for child support and maybe I'll be able to get by." The idea of taking alimony repulsed me. I considered it charity and besides, he kept making dirty remarks about "parasites" who bled their poor husbands.*
>
> *Then the word got to me that he was having an extremely extensive social life. This woman, that woman. Apparently he was having a fine time. I thought, "He's spending the money on other women. Better it should be me. I've earned it."*
>
> *For seven years I kept his house, washed his clothes, cooked his meals, raised his children, and entertained his pissy friends. Once we were separated, his share of the money allowed him to blow $30 on a dinner date and my share allowed me to treat the kids to a $3.47 dinner at the Burger King.*
>
> *I decided to roast him and the place to start was with alimony.*

Judy, a self-styled alimoniac and proud of it, believes she is doing her husband a favor:

> *When I married him I had the beginnings of a fairly respectable career as a fashion illustrator. He insisted I quit because a working wife didn't fit his image as a successful businessman and Kiwanis Club member. Now I was supposed to pick up where I left off eight years ago and earn my own living again. Even if it had been possible, which I doubt, I still would have said, "Hell no, buster."*
>
> *Why should I? He clears close to $60,000 a year. He doesn't miss the $15,000. From any way you look at it, he's in the catbird seat because he's got a gorgeous tax break. He should thank me.*
>
> *I tried to get him for $20,000. I told myself, "This is the biggest business deal you'll ever make. If you play it smart, you'll be set for life."*

Our Children. After a husband surveys the damage to his exchequer, naturally he feels like a chump. He promptly moves to protect what's left of his property. Usually his wife beats him to the household artifacts. Libby hired a mover:

> *Instead of giving me a big wedding, my parents bought all our furniture as a wedding gift. So there was no dispute about dividing. It was all mine and I took it.*

So much for *our* furniture. But a couple's most valuable joint holding is children. A wife is astonished to learn that her husband regards them as part of his permanent assets. Considering that his relationship with the children has been limited to a few minutes of play after dinner, that is, on those nights he makes it home for dinner, one would think he'd be happy with the status quo. But no. Now he fervently insists that he wants custody, a fancy way to say motherhood. Aware that the last thing Daddy desires is to be a mother, a wife calls his bluff by acing him with Father Goose, a delightfully dirty game she can improvise as she goes along.

Unknown to Daddy, the life of a custodial parent has a few minor drawbacks. Aside from the discouraging fact that she has $21.55 left of her weekly pay-check after deducting carfare, lunches, and baby-sitter, the custodian is, to use a polite term, tied down. When her work day is over, she can't, in contrast to Daddy, pop into the nearest cocktail lounge for a leisurely evening of dissipation. She rushes home to dismiss the baby-sitter or to collect her kids from whosoever's house they've been tearing apart. Her evenings are spent cooking, cleaning, laundering, storytelling, bathing, and supervising homework. When she goes out for an evening, it means paying another baby-sitter. Nor can she take advantage of Daddy's favorite recreation after martinis: a warm body in his bed all night.

Custody, however, is what Daddy claims he wants. Giving it to him is one way to play Father Goose. Denise explains why she was willing:

> *He believed I should bring him coffee in the morning, he believed I should cook for him, and he believed I should have a baby so that he could be a father. Since he wanted a baby so badly, I think it's only fair for him to keep Bobby.*
>
> *Of course, now what's happened is that he resents my freedom. That's why he wants me to pay him child support. To punish me a little. If he looked for ways to work it out, I'm sure he could have* almost *as much freedom as I do. If he really wants a child of his own, then he must realize that being tied down is the price.*

In most cases when a Daddy insists on custody, he has something up his sleeve, and it's invariably a new woman. Amanda muses upon her replacement:

> *Recently he told me that he's changed his mind and now he'd like to have custody of Karin. He said he wants to raise her but I don't think that's it at all.*

Now he's living with another woman and I hear they're going to have a child in June. He figures she might as well take care of two children while she's at it. I wonder how she feels?

When Daddy lived at home, the most useful function he served was paying the children's bills. Now that he's gone, a wife continues to regard him as a checkbook. Besides, his newfound interest in the children aggravates her:

1. He uses his visitation privileges to snoop around her house and read her mail.
2. Seeing as how he refused to sign a separation agreement which would have obligated him to pay for orthodontia, she healthily mistrusts his love.
3. Despite his request for custody, she notices his visits becoming fewer and less regular. What's more, the support checks seem to be getting lost in the mail more frequently.

The typical wife simply allows father nature to take its course. She silently stands by as Daddy gumshoes his way out of her and her children's lives and disappears into a second marriage and a new family. Leah didn't wait for time to take care of Daddy's shenanigans. She handled the situation herself:

At no time did Harry show an overabundance of love for Jason. I got the feeling that he regarded the child as a piece of property.

His visits grew extremely erratic. Either he was late or he wouldn't show up at all. Then I noticed he wasn't paying Jason's medical bills. And then he stopped sending support money. He said he didn't have it but he did have enough to dress well and vacation in Mexico. Finally I'd had it: "You don't have money for Jason, then I don't have time for Jason to see you."

For months after that, he threatened to kidnap Jason and beat me up and kill me. I was petrified but I refused to let him in the house. In the end it was my attorney who sold me down the river by making a deal with Harry's lawyer. For $15 a week Harry could see Jason every other week. By this time it had been thirteen months. Jason didn't even remember him.

Harry and I and the two attorneys met in my lawyer's office. I said to them, "Harry threatened to kill me and kidnap Jason. And now you want me to let him visit?" My ex-husband replied, "Sure I threatened you but I didn't mean it." In front of my lawyer he admitted it and still my lawyer didn't say a word. The meeting ended with their *decision that Harry would be around at 3 o'clock on Saturday. This was a Monday.*

"Nobody is going to help you," I said to myself. "Better use self-help." The only solution I could think of was for me and Jason to disappear. Vanishing had occurred to me before and I'd investigated the possibility of renting a house and hiding for a few months. I'd even looked at a place in Jersey but it was too expensive.

Since Jersey was out I went to Belgium. I had friends there with whom I'd be safe. Harry wouldn't dream that I'd leave the country.

From my lawyer's office, I went directly to Pan Am and bought a ticket for Friday evening.

When I returned two months later, I remarried and moved out of town. I haven't heard from Harry since.

Male Chauvinist Pig Attorneys. The prototype for your male chauvinist pig may very well be a divorce lawyer. At any rate, divorcees rarely have anything good to say about the lot. A woman retains an attorney because she's desperate, meaning she wants to learn where next month's rent is coming from. The other thing she needs is hard-nosed professional advice to fill in the gaps of her do-it-yourself law studies. Her expectation that an attorney will fill these needs turns out to be wildly unreasonable. Instead, she seems to be face-to-face with a voyeur who ignores her financial difficulties and keeps steering the conversation to irrelevancies:

> *MCP: "What happened?"*
> *Client: "Whaddaya mean, 'What happened?'"*
> *MCP: "What happened to make you and your husband separate?"*
> *Client: "(........)"*

No more able to level with him than her husband, she manages to come up with an explanation which not only sounds reasonable but fits one of the grounds for divorce in her state. This seems to signal the start of a new game but exactly what game is unclear as yet. As the initial conference proceeds, her attorney analyzes the cause of her marital failure, cross-examines her about past and present sexual activities, and delivers a short lecture on child-rearing. By the time he pats her on the head and sends her home, she's mapped out the necessary game, Orphan of the Storm. Nora spotted the possibilities before she retained an attorney:

> *After Roy had been gone a few months, the super of my building remarked: "How's the mister? Haven't seen him for awhile."*
>
> *"Oh him," I answered. "He doesn't live here anymore."*
>
> *Mr. Sanchez looked terribly upset: "I'm sorry. If there's anything I can do ..."*
>
> *I was going to tell him I wasn't a bit sorry but he probably would have had an attack. He acted as though some catastrophe had befallen me.*
>
> *"Hold on," I said to myself, "If he feels so sorry for you, I'll bet you can get him to do a few repairs*

for a change." And I began to make a mental list of things which needed fixing.

Judy demonstrates how she invented Orphan of the Storm:

> *I'd heard enough about divorce lawyers to realize it was easy to get stuck with a pig. So I decided to shop around before I plunked down a retainer fee. The time and money were well-spent because I learned the basic rule of the game. Divorce attorneys fall into two categories: those who hate women and those who regard us as simps. The important thing is to make sure you hire one of the latter.*
>
> *You wear your sexiest outfit, put the tears on standby, and sail into his office prepared with your tearjerker tale. In the last reel, you throw yourself at his feet. That's what they expect*
>
> *It was sickening but I did it.*

A woman hardly expects a male lawyer to be a fervent partisan for the female sex, but, at the very least, she assumes he will work for her. This is not the case. Her suspicions may be first aroused when she overhears a telephone conversation between her attorney and the opposing counsel; it sounds like they're in cahoots. Her counsel reminds her of his policy which is "to settle these matters as amicably as possible." Now she knows there's trouble ahead.

Before long, the male booster club is operating in its usual fashion. Not only is her attorney hunkering with the opposition, but soon it's impossible to distinguish her attorney from her husband's. And, in fact, both men are working for the same team: his. It's not hard to figure out the reason. In most states, courts customarily direct the husband to pay his wife's counsel fees, a custom recognizing the wife's penniless condition. Saddled with an attorney working in her husband's best interests, a wife relies on Orphan of the Storm to prevent being sold all the way down the river instead of only half way. Angela's tale reveals a clear portrait of the male chauvinist pig divorce attorney. Welcome to him:

> *When I first met him, I thought, "This is what I've always imagined a bookie to look like." From then on, I referred to him as Harry the Horse. He was a horsey-faced gentleman in his fifties, with greased-down hair, a perpetual tan, gold fillings, and expensive checked suits. But since he'd been highly recommended, I decided to overlook his not being a sex object. As it turned out, he was an authentic repulsive in nearly every way. I was involved with that shyster pig for over a year—that's how long it took me to get a divorce—and I despised him. But I couldn't fire him because he'd extorted a $300 retainer fee on my first visit and I knew he'd never return it. I'd scraped together the three hundred bucks by selling my books and closing my secret bank account of money purloined from my grocery allowance when I'd been married. I simply didn't have the money to start over with a new lawyer.*
>
> *The second meeting I smelled something rotten. I wasn't quite sure but it sounded as though he was insulting me. I remember smiling nervously, not being able to believe my ears. When I left the office, it sunk in. I was enraged! I wanted to kill and there was no one to kill. He had said to me, "I ought to turn you over my knee and give you a good spanking." The reason for that remark was a letter I had written to my husband, graphically describing how I planned to flatten his pocketbook. It seemed that he showed the letter to his attorney who promptly called Harry the Horse and they enjoyed a huge laugh over it. "What do you want to do?" grinned Harry the Horse, with his thousands of gold teeth flashing. "Crucify the poor*

guy?" That was all I needed. From then on, it was me against the three of them.

From everything I had read or heard, I knew I was asking the bare minimum from my husband. But not according to Harry the Horse. He was always quoting some judge or other: "Judge So-and-So would consider $15 a week an inordinate amount of child support." Or he'd say, "You don't want alimony. You should get a full-time job."

What I hated most was his prying into my sex life. He wanted to know if I were sleeping around. Even though I said "No," he gave me a lecture on a mother's morals. When it came to a father's morals, that was different. I had wanted to sue on the grounds of adultery; it was the most obvious ground because my husband was living with a woman, but Harry the Horse wouldn't hear of it "If your husband didn't have a woman, I'd think he was queer," he said. Apparently he believed fucking was normal for a separated man but not for a separated woman.

Every time I saw him, spoke to him, or thought of him, I felt murderous.

I don't know who I loathed more, him or my husband. I guess it was a toss-up.

III. THERAPY GAMES

Character Assassination. After the keystone comedy of divorce, a woman needs therapy badly. But at precisely the moment when she could use a psychiatrist, such frivolity is out of the question. Thanks to The Breadwinner's miserliness with *our* money, she couldn't afford treatment even if she stole from her children's support money. As a matter of fact, she's pilfering from it anyway for personal necessities like babysitters. She must look for other outlets to release the wrath left unexpressed to her husband.

For that matter, what about telling her ex-husband the reason she divorced him? Certainly it would be a cheaper method of drawing and quartering him than paying $35 an hour to a shrink who wouldn't be able to fully appreciate her motives anyway. The childless woman may attempt the direct method of getting it out of her system once and for all, but even she comes to realize its futility; her ex-husband doesn't comprehend one-tenth of her story. Honest carnage may also tempt the divorced mother. For Nora, the moment of truth came and went:

> *One evening a few months after the divorce, he brought Andrea home and settled down with a whiskey just as if he were still master of the house. "I want to talk to you," he said. And then he started on a monologue about people learning from their mistakes. Finally he got to the point: "Why were you so determined to split us up? I'd like to know because I might marry again and I don't want to make the same mistake twice."*
>
> *"Well, now's the chance," I thought. "He's asking for it." But I found I couldn't. I didn't know where to begin. And if I told him the truth, he might melt in a puddle before my eyes. I guess I pitied him.*
>
> *So I answered, "People change over the years and sometimes they grow in different directions. Why don't we just let it go at that?"*

For a divorced woman, however, there is no such concept as bygones. Unable to admit she's a bit immature in this respect, she turns to a hastily refined version of Don't Rock the Boat: No Hard Feelings. She has serious practical reasons for game playing because she depends on her ex-husband's money for survival. A Daddy may be legally obligated for his wife and children's support, but she has heard enough scare stories to know the grizzly pranks he can pull with the monthly allotment: checks lost in the mail, bounced checks, bills never received, trips to Family Court to collect an overdue $65, additional legal fees just to learn that a forgetful Daddy has been lolling on the beach in St. Thomas, and the classic situation where the check arrives later and later until Daddy is able to sneak in a free month. Although a certain percentage of these calamities will happen no matter what, she takes every precaution to head them off. If she is careful not to rile her ex-husband, maybe she will be lucky.

No Hard Feelings is necessary for another reason. Children of divorce need to know their father still loves them, and it's a Mother's duty, or so it says in *Parents' Magazine,* to foster a good relationship. Personally, she fails to see why her children need any relationship with a viper like her ex-husband, but obviously this attitude is anathema. She is hard put to say anything good about him, but at least she refrains from saying anything vile in her children's presence. For that matter, running down Daddy would only result in a backlash which she doesn't need because the kids won't pay attention to her now anyway. Although she can't prove it, she suspects he uses his visitation time to paint her as The Wicked Witch of the West. Even if he isn't smearing her in so many words, his battle for property rights continues as he plies the kids with:

1. Items she forbids, bubble gum to name one.
2. $12.50 front row seats to the circus.
3. Taxi rides.
4. $100 birthday bikes.

Save for the bubble gum, none of these items can be covered on the money he gives her to feed, clothe, and house the children, a fact about which he is all too happily aware. Daddy also knows that she makes a lot of idiotic demands such as bathing and teethbrushing. When the children visit him, these rules are promptly suspended. As a result, the kids believe Daddy is a swell guy after all and Mother is a first-class tightwad and martinet. The thought which sustains her through this treacherous period is that someday the children will be smart enough to see he's a rat.

For the moment, however, she works on developing her capacity for cordiality. At the same time, though, her fury is mounting to new heights, not only for past crimes but for the rotten tricks he's presently pulling. One place she can take care of him as she'd like is in the privacy of her fantasies:

> *LIBBY - During the separation period I never said nasty things about him. I even recall saying nice things. That's because I was afraid of him. But I used to dream of ways to kill him. My favorite was a truck running over him. I'd lure him to a deserted spot on the highway and wait until a trailer truck approached. Then I'd push. He'd be squashed. Completely obliterated.*

> *NORA - I wanted him to disappear, anything so that I'd never need to see him again. Or sometimes I'd tell myself, "He's going to suddenly die at the age of forty-five." I should be so lucky.*

> *ANGELA - When Harry the Horse was rehearsing me for the court appearance and I was going over my testimony, I had this wonderful thought. I would say, "Judge, my husband has this disturbing habit. He pees the bed."*

> *LEAH - When he was threatening to kidnap Jason, I think I would have killed him if I'd been able to get away with it As a kid, I remember my brother telling me about a foolproof method. You inject a needleful of air into the jugular vein and then you scratch the person with his own fingertip so the puncture mark is hidden. Then you cover it with a Band Aid so it looks like the person scratched himself. And you're home free.*

Unfortunately, Harry was too big for me to subdue and my aim is pretty bad. Also I didn't have the nerve. Also I didn't want his death on my conscience.

While fantasizing is helpful, character assassination remains the divorcee's chief means of therapy. She avails herself of this treatment practically every time she mentions her ex-husband's name. As the last thing her women friends expect is kind reminiscences, she's free to express her honest opinions as often as she likes.

LEAH - *The night I left him, I wiped out five years of my life in a few hours. There was no period of transition. It was as if our marriage had never been. I had no recollection of having ever loved him.*

During the first few months of separation, I felt numb: I didn't like him or dislike him. He became so unimportant in my life that he didn't merit an emotion. This was followed by a period when I grew to dislike him intensely and from there I went on to despising and eventually to hating him.

Now he simply disgusts me. If he were an animal, I'd destroy him for his own sake.

NORA - *I've heard of couples who grow friendly after they divorce. In my case, it's been four years without this happening. I doubt if it ever will.*

When he first left, I felt somewhat kindly but that was simply relief and gratitude over his moving. As time went on I realized how much hostility I truly had. A lot.

If it weren't for my daughter, I would have made sure I never saw him again.

DENISE - *Some days of the week I hate him. Other days I hate him only indirectly. I mean, things will come up—like sex—and I realize he's responsible for the way I feel. Thanks to the sexual experiences I had with him, I had begun to feel that sex was awful.*

Nora's Diary.

Saturday, October 26—Tonight I'm alone. Andrea is with her father. In three weeks and two days I'll be thirty-five. All evening I've been thinking about where I'm going but I must force myself to write it. I'm afraid to dream on paper. I ask myself, "What do I want?" I've never seriously thought about this before, but now I must.

I want money. Enough so I don't have to worry, or watch every cent, or drive myself crazy when Roy's check is late. I want Andrea to be a few years older and more of a companion so that I can be less of a Mommy. Andrea, Andrea... I hope she won't hate me too much. Someday I hope she will understand me and love me for what I am. I denied her a mommy-daddy-baby-makes-three life but I hope I can give her something better. I want a different kind of life for my daughter, not the woman's life I have. I fear that it won't be possible though. Why must each one of us live through the identical pain her mother suffered? From generation to generation, the cycle is unbroken. We blindfold ourselves so eagerly. We ignore, we discount, we will be different from Mother. Each woman starts anew, as if she were Eve. Is there no way I can warn Andrea? Save her?

I want Roy in my graveyard of men I've loved. A curious memory.

I want to live without turmoil. Emotionless. Calm. The scars healed. My body no longer a battlefield. I want myself back again. My thoughts. My life. My name. What else? To be whole, nerveless, confident, in control, my brain unparalyzed. I want to be the way I was as a girl. Now that it's possible

> *to build a life of my own, I hardly know where to start. But at least I've begun. I see the outline of the structure slowly coming into focus. The interior remains empty.*
>
> *It takes so long.*

Reflections on One's Future. Divorce returns a woman to GO. By marrying and bearing children she has paid her dues. Now she feels entitled to do as she pleases, make up for the lost years as Mrs. Whatshisname, and become her own person again, whoever that may be. Her first item of business is dropping *our* friends. Amanda recalls:

> *The friends we had were his friends. When we separated, I had to reestablish relationships with old friends who hadn't liked him or whom he hadn't liked. I hadn't seen much of those people while I was married.*

The most important matter, however, is to reestablish contact with the enemy forces. Despite her unfortunate experience, she allows herself to feel new optimism about mankind. It's always possible her ex-husband was the only no-good apple in the barrel. Embarking on a rediscovery tour of the male sex, she begins dating only to run smack into The Man Problem once more. This time the situation is complicated by a brand-new factor: The men she meets are either thirty-five-year-old bachelors living with their mothers or randy divorced Daddies. The former only want a live audience for airing their misadventures with Mama, the latter a chance to reconstruct the mysterious circumstances leading up to the explosion of their marriages.

At any rate, one encouraging surprise is finding that a divorced Daddy promises to be fairly virile. After the crucifixion his manhood suffered at the hands of his ex-wife, Daddy is psychologically primed for a sexual renaissance. However, the main reason he furiously sleeps around is that he hates to go home at night. The bed is unmade, a week's worth of dirty dishes wait in the sink, and he's afraid of the dark. At bedtime he must have his blanket and bottle, a night light, a teddy bear, in short, a woman.

The divorced mother inadequately fills a divorced Daddy's sexual needs because she can't sleep the entire night at his place, nor can she permit him bunking in with her. Either way, the kids tend to talk. But that's not the only problem; five, ten, or twenty years of non-sex sex has sabotaged much of the mystique of lovemaking. Nor is it so easy to play the old romantic vamping games. Now that nobody can call her an "old maid," she is less willing to go out of her way to please a man. What men think of her becomes less important than what she thinks of them. Denise finds her new attitude toward men, both in and out of bed, somewhat disturbing:

> *One night I slept with this man and we had a fine time. The next morning I went to visit my son. Usually I don't wake my husband but this particular morning, there was something I wanted to tell Barney. I shook his shoulder and said, "Sweetheart." Then I thought, "Oh, fuck it. What am I doing?" Because the man no longer makes any difference to me. When I'm feeling good, all men are sweethearts; when I'm feeling bad, they're all schmucks.*
>
> *I look at them as sex objects. There's one guy with whom I've been having a really hot affair. But we have very little conversation. Mostly we play giggle games. Once I told him my fantasy: that he should come to my apartment, ring the bell, come inside, fuck me, and then leave. The whole time he shouldn't say one word.*
>
> *Now maybe he thought, "Wow, this chick is just too selfish. She's treating me like a thing." But he didn't question my fantasy.*
>
> *I think it's a real failure on my part to treat a man*

as a component of my fantasies. But that's where I'm at and it's going to take a while to overcome it.

The last thing a divorcee wants is to become a hermit. After years of Better Homes and Gardened purdah, years relieved now and then by a maid's night out with The Breadwinner, she longs for dancing, restaurant dinners, nights at the theater. Since these days she has little patience with what people think, she'd be delighted to step out with a woman friend. But now most of her friends are married, which means they are busy doing nightly waitress duty for their breadwinners. In many ways, then, her second life as a single woman is more disturbing than the first. She still needs a man. Or does she? Judy dryly examines the available substitutes:

Sometimes I simply feel I don't want anything to do with men. Under what circumstances I will have sex with a woman, I don't know. But eventually I'll do it. I'm much more intimate with women than any man I'm sleeping with now. However, that's not where my friends' heads are at. It would have to be someone new. I'm sure I'll meet someone and it will happen. I want enough options so that sex will be possible without my having to marry again.

It's going to take me a long time to decide what kind of a relationship I want with a man. The first time Carl said, "Fix me a sandwich," I should have answered, "Fuck off and fix your own sandwich." Now I wouldn't cook for a man for all the money in the world.

Sooner or later there's no way to avoid the troublesome, pivotal question: does she want to remarry? Knowing what she does about marriage and husbands, Angela believes not. Which creates more conflicts than it resolves:

A psychic who read my cards saw a ring in my future. "No doubt about it," she told me, "You'll marry again." The prediction made me furious because I thought, "Maybe she's right. Maybe I would be stupid enough to go through it all again." Most days I feel positive I'll never remarry simply because I've reached a point of no return with men. I could never wait on one again.

I mean, I don't really like men as people. I've never known one who I would consider a whole human being. But then I think, "What about sex? I need men." If I eliminate men, what am I left with? Other women, masturbation, celibacy. I don't see any satisfactory solution. I say to myself, "Well, Angela, it's men or nothing. So snap out of it and stop acting like a freak."

If worst comes to worst, and ultimately it does, a woman decides to give marriage another try. As always, the problem is money. After all, as Libby points out, a woman must look ahead to her sunset years:

I consider myself a happily divorced woman. But then I think of the future and it's a nightmare. What will happen to me when I'm seventy or eighty? I won't have a husband's retirement income or a widow's insurance. I can't save anything out of my salary now. What will I do in thirty years? So I always keep one eye open for a husband.

A divorcee runs her life on a shoestring; little wonder that money and the lack of it is her favorite topic. Denise isn't concerned about money for her old age. It's forty that bothers her:

I can't think ahead to my old age. I'm worried about what will become of me when I'm forty. Or next year. What if I lose this job? What if my

> *husband dies? What if I have to take care of my kid?*
>
> *Now I live a minimal existence but how long can I go on? I have three pairs of corduroy pants. I wheedle dinners out of people. The way I spend money is not to spend it. People say to me, "Don't you want a nice apartment and nice furniture and nice clothes?"*
>
> *Maybe I've decided on this ascetic life so I don't have to make a lot of money. I don't know.*
>
> *Well, I'll just wait and see what happens.*

On the other hand, there's this to consider: A divorcee is a seasoned professional when it comes to marriage. Any institution supplying free room and board can't be all bad. Maybe next time she can sidestep the worst booby traps. Perhaps her husband will be able to afford a paid live-in maid. After several years of penny-pinching freedom, she almost looks forward to a resumption of the old political games with a new husband. Why let all that hard-earned experience go to waste?

If Little Darling remarries, her second term in the institution may be easier. If not, she resigns herself because she's too old to voluntarily face the hardships of a single woman's life for a third time. The comforting thought is that old age is near. The risk she takes is dying before her husband and thus missing out on the joys of widowhood. Statistically, however, the smart money is on her.

SEVEN

You've Come a Long Way, Baby

I. GERIATRIC GAMES
- Leftover Objects
- Old Massa
- Last Rites

II. LIBERATION
- Elegies to His Memory
- If I Had My Life to Live Over

You've Come a Long Way, Baby

As a woman approaches her Golden Age, the conflicts with her husband simmer down into a war of attrition: small guerrilla skirmishes, swift lunges below the belt, unexpected tongue lashings. She's apt to grow a shade careless in the backstretch because she knows that now it's more or less a matter of time. Nevertheless, the games will be formally called only on account of death. If this leaves men feeling slightly nervous, here's another grotesque thought: What will your wife say about you when you've gone?

Look at this closing chapter as the last word in bitching.

I. GERIATRIC GAMES

Leftover Objects. Little Darling discharged her obligation some time back. Defined from birth by her reproductive organs, she seemed eager to accommodate the adults who presented her with glassy eyed, neutered dolls. So enthusiastically did she dress and cuddle them that people said she was born for it. Admittedly, she longed for their transformation into real babies, but, confronted with her own for the first time, little wonder she resented their excretory organs, a footnote to the motherhood story the doll-makers had conveniently censored. Still, preordination is not a matter for argument, and she cheerfully filled her uterus once, twice, or as many times as necessary. By now, however, the by-products of her destiny have long since fled. For that matter, she's lucky if she even owns a uterus because some overzealous gynecologist most likely has given her a hysterectomy whether she needed one or not.

With or without uterus, she still has a body which now is more of a problem than ever. While she continues to masquerade as a Little Darling, indeed may even still feel like a Little Darling inside, she no longer looks like one. One of her main social uses had been as a human ornament standing around ready to be ravished. Although her husband, no broth of a boy himself, still refers to her as a girl, her value as a sex object is zero. Worthless in men's eyes, therefore worthless as a human being, she frantically tries to reverse her slide into the female garbage heap with Clairol rinses and Warner's latest miracle cure for flabby belly and waffled thighs. All her life she had been exhorted by the fashion and cosmetic industries to step right up and pick an image. True, her selection was limited to one of two choices, siren or little girl, but it kept her busy. Now that sagging breasts disqualify her to be a siren, she is stuck with the little girl look, an image good for all ages.

If her season as a sex object is ended, her life as a sexual person also appears done for. After thirty years or more as a wife, she no longer complains about her husband's inadequacies in bed. The woman now in her sixties or seventies never had much of a sex life to miss. Orgasm is a meaningless word for Becky:

> *I may have had one once. I never thought about orgasms; certainly I never imagined it was my husband's responsibility to see that I enjoyed myself in bed. Sex wasn't something I discussed with Max. I just did it.*
>
> *I grew up with the idea that it was a wife's duty to sleep with her husband. One reason I didn't want to get married was I thought a wife had to perform this duty every night.*

The older woman's attitude toward sex and the people with whom one performed this clandestine activity was fashioned in the pre-Sexual Revolutionary era. As a result her views on conjugal passion sound remarkably old-fashioned, as Gertrude's comments illustrate:

> *I thought of a husband as a hard, burly stranger who had a tube attached to him. He stuck it in you twice a week if you were lucky, every night if you weren't.*

But for the wife of many years, sexuality has ceased to be a problem. Florence, retired from the arena, contributes a report on the sex life of her husband:

> *My interest in sex was smothered ages ago. It's been years since Will and I slept in the same room. I don't know what he does for sex and I don't care. He looks, I guess. Not at me, of course, at girls. He's a dirty old man.*
>
> *I see him peering down the blouses of my daughters-in-law, staring at waitresses and salesgirls. As long as he doesn't bother me, he can get his thrills where he likes. When he rides me over to the shopping center, I'll go to Sears and he disappears. I know he sneaks off to the pharmacy where they've got dirty magazines but I never let on. I could split my sides laughing.*

One compensation for the departure of children, bless their hearts, is that Mother gets something she's dreamed about for years: a room of her own. Nellie felt rejuvenated:

> *When Barbara left, I moved into her room. It was nice having my own room and my own bed again. It made me feel like a little girl. Even now, I stretch and roll from one side of the bed to the other and pull the covers over my head and keep the light on until two o'clock if I feel like it.*

Unfortunately, she can no longer count on the sensual joys of shopping as an erotic outlet because once The Breadwinner retires, there is usually less money to spend. If anybody deserves to use it, he does. After all, he's worked hard all his life. Now he'd like to indulge himself a bit. Of course, if the Senior Citizen, a euphemism for Head of Household, decides to move to a warmer climate, the Assistant Senior Citizen stands to benefit also. Not, mind you, that this is his motivation. On the other hand, should she feel reluctant about leaving friends and home, she is forced to tag along anyway.

The marriage contract double-crossed her in more ways than one. It saddled her with a job from which there is no retirement Although The Breadwinner is retired, she still has plenty of housework to do because her lifetime pilgrimage in search of a paid maid rarely ends in success. Another dream down the drain she's Dranoed for half a century. Florence tried to negotiate a last-minute retirement policy:

> *I saw a brochure for a retirement village, one of those places where they have nice little apartments. They provide your linens and a maid comes around to clean. The apartments had cute little kitchens with dishwashers. The place even had a restaurant if you didn't feel like cooking.*
>
> *I said to Will, "Let's give up this barn. We don't need it anymore." Nobody uses half the rooms but they still have to be cleaned. He said, "I've lived in this house thirty years and it's my home. I'm not going to live in a closet." What does he care about dishwashers and maids? But what he says, goes.*

After an eternity of boiling eggs to suit The Breadwinner's specifications, the cook is ready to explode. But she puts on a happy face as she continues to do the housewife's goosestep.

Old Massa. The home which tradition and the male establishment designated as her place suddenly ceases to be a sanctuary; once her husband retires, it signals the invasion and occupation of her kingdom. At first this might look like the start of a housewife's New Deal. Now that he can't use his work as an excuse, he might be willing to help out more often around the house. Maybe cook once in a while, do the marketing, defrost the refrigerator. It's certainly worth investigating. She quickly learns, however, that a person accustomed to a lifetime of guaranteed service will not easily accept its curtailment or termination. One evening Ruth attempted to deliver a cutoff notice:

> *I've got arthritis in both hands. Some days it gets so bad I can hardly iron or turn on the stove. One night I remember saying to Leon, "I don't think I'm gonna be able to cook tonight." I knew he'd never offer to fix dinner but I figured maybe he'd bring in some Chinese food. "Oh, that's okay," he says. "You can just make me a sandwich."*

At this stage of the game, a wife can afford to remain stoic. A sandwich isn't worth a head-on confrontation when it's only a matter of time until circumstance discharges her as a cook. Meanwhile she plays the treasured family political games less patiently. An expert at flattening Gramps' ego, she concentrates on fast verbal workouts which she knows from experience she can win. While blistering him regularly with sassy contempt, she continues to serve him after a fashion. Irene disdained such rookie games as Keeping One's Mouth Shut:

> *He'd poke his nose into my kitchen and start to rearrange the groceries in the pantry. It seemed he didn't like the way I organized the shelves. Or he'd complain the toaster was full of crumbs or the electric broiler felt greasy. I'd scream, "Who do you think you are? A health inspector? If my kitchen isn't clean enough to suit you, eat someplace else."*

Gertrude washed her husband's shirts, but she put her feelings out to dry alongside:

> *I can hear him now: "A man shouldn't have to ask for a clean shirt." Or he'd yell, "This collar is wrinkled." Oh, he imagined himself a real fancy Dan. He was always hollering about his clothes. The older he got, the more particular he became. But I didn't take any crap from him. "I've been ironing forty years," I told him. "You don't like the way I do shirts, take 'em to the laundry." What a joke! He was too cheap.*
>
> *I stood up to him.*

A wife's final game with The Breadwinner is Life Insurance. It requires her to demonstrate, come what may, the fealty of a loving wife until death do them part. This means serving him three meals a day instead of two, scheduling her housework around his favorite television programs, and reconciling herself to the fact that his demands upon her will be increasing. In other words, her declining years are rewarded with a brand-new baby. Lillian furnishes an index to the care and feeding of a retired husband:

> *I couldn't get used to having Mack around the house all day. It was worse than having a baby underfoot. He was making me crazy. For example, he didn't like me to run the sweeper because he couldn't hear the television. He had the nerve to ask, "Can't you vacuum later?" At breakfast he'd cozy up to me and say, "Howzabout some griddle cakes this morning?" Like every day was Sunday.*
>
> *Since he made friends with a couple of old fogeys like himself, he spends more of the day drinking coffee with them. I told him, "Don't bring those bums over here. Go sit in the park or go to the cafeteria." When he's home, he sits in front of the television. In the evening, I play Scrabble with him for awhile and then he goes back to the TV. At eleven o'clock, he wants a glass of milk and a*

liverwurst sandwich to eat while he watches the news. After that he goes to bed.

And that's what it's like every day around here.

As in the days of her first pregnancy when she believed a baby would be the panacea for loneliness, a woman may temporarily con herself into imagining a husband around the house could provide company. Florence tried to reverse a lifetime of non-conversation conversation:

> *In one way I looked forward to his being home because I'd have someone to talk to. "Will," I said, "at our age we should talk more." But I'm the one who talks. I wouldn't ever call them conversations. The only folks he talks to are his pals.*
>
> *I've been living with him forty-two years. What more can I say? It sure ain't been no picnic. He's never asked me what I thought about anything. I used to tell myself it's because he doesn't think to ask but I finally decided he didn't* care *what I thought.*
>
> *His work always came first. That was made clear when we married. I remember the day Jackie was born and I wanted him to take the day off and stay with me at the hospital. Mercy no, his business was too important to leave for one day. He went off and left me alone.*
>
> *Now that he's been retired four years, he doesn't have work to occupy him anymore. Now it's his golf and his cards and his beery cronies. Something always comes before me.*

One of the distinguishing features of a husband is his helplessness. Now, however, there may be a good cause. Sooner or later, he suffers from poor health or various degrees of incapacitation. (His wife may not feel any too well either, but she stumbles through the housework anyway.) As a consequence, his last years may call for special diets, medicine, and care. If he should require a nurse, he turns to his own private duty nursing staff: his wife. She often feels compassion for him—and then again she may not. Either way, duty and Life Insurance impel her to oblige. Pearl failed to appreciate her new nursing career:

> *He had prostate trouble and had to have an operation. The way he carried on when he was sick! Like a child who's always calling for Mommy. He couldn't do anything for himself. I had to coax him to take his medicine and eat what the doctor ordered. Mostly what I remember from that time is fixing trays. And jumping up when he called me.*
>
> *It was a struggle to keep from going loony.*

Ordinarily, a wife entering the intoxicating final dash has enough savvy to keep going. This doesn't mean, however, that the idea of dropping out doesn't cross her mind. At the age of sixty, Gertrude studied the rewards of divorce before she temporarily shelved the solution:

> *My mother suffered a good deal in her marriage but her attitude was, marriage isn't easy. If you can't get along with the man you've chosen, it's your tough luck. I'd always gone along with that theory but I began to change my mind.*
>
> *When the kids were living at home. Nelson and I got on pretty well. It was understood that each of us had our own business to tend. He was a snotty old bastard but I didn't pay him any mind. After my daughter married and my son moved to California, that's when the trouble started. It was rough being alone with him and it got so we were always fighting.*
>
> *He had a bad temper. Once when he'd been laid off for six months, he got pretty vicious. Everything bad that happened to him, he blamed on me.*
>
> *"You're still a young woman," I told myself, "You want to go completely out of your mind?" I was*

> *about sixty then. At the back of my mind, I decided to divorce him. But I didn't say anything to him.*
>
> *My friend Emma was very much opposed. "Asinine" was what she called it because if I divorced him, I'd wind up with nothing. "Wait," she said, "I've got a feeling that everything will work out all right." A strange thing but Emma was always getting feelings about things and a lot of the time, she turned out to be right. But this time I didn't trust her feeling. She was talking like Nelson was going to die soon and I knew positively there was nothing wrong with him.*

Last Rites. Abruptly, Life Insurance draws to a close. No longer a wife, the widow finds that her career as a housewife is over as well. The live-in maid is dismissed, laid off, set free. Her first emotion, however, is neither grief nor the fear she will experience shortly when she faces life as a single woman once more. Her primary worry, as always, is survival. Like the wife contemplating divorce, she conducts a full-scale postmortem on bank books, stock certificates, and life insurance policies. For the first time, *our* money is no longer his. Before redistributing the wealth, however, she needs to establish whether it's *hers,* as opposed to that of various creditors or the government.

While furiously auditing the books, she pays her final respects to the deceased with the last game she may ever have to play, My Husband Was a Wonderful Man. Becky's memory of her husband's death includes a brief description of the game:

> *I was lonely and terribly afraid.*
>
> *The morning he died, I locked myself in my room and wouldn't open the door. I remember my son pounding on the door until I thought he meant to break it in. "Go away," I finally yelled. "I'll come out when I'm goddammed good and ready." He must have been so shocked to hear me swearing*

> *that he left. At eight o'clock that evening I went downstairs and started making calls.*
>
> *The worst part was talking to people. They'd say, "Max was a wonderful man," and I'd answer, "Yes, my husband was a wonderful man." I must have repeated those words a thousand times before he was buried. And all the time I kept thinking, "You didn't know him like I did. He wasn't such a wonderful man." And because I felt terrible thinking that way, I'd make excuses and tell myself it was the shock of his passing. I wasn't myself.*

Until the last moment, she dutifully served him, but the irony is, she must continue to care for him when he's dead.

Of course she has a perfect excuse to withdraw, and many women do. If children or relatives will handle arrangements for the last rites, she can arrange a convenient collapse by retreating into womanly vapors. Otherwise, she must tidy up his death as she did his life. Pearl efficiently buried her second husband, Mr. Gallagher, except for one slip:

> *I handled all the arrangements myself. I was surprised that I could manage everything so well on my own. Before the casket was closed, I peeked at him for a last time. Suddenly I realized I was sort of giggling and it horrified me so that I began to cry. Very loud.*

Two factors stopped Gertrude from pursuing a divorce: her husband's insurance and her friend Emma's "feeling." Now for the surprise ending:

> *Maybe I did kind of believe Emma because I didn't leave him. Instead, the following April I decided I deserved a vacation from him. I had a little money put by, enough to go on a bus tour to Washington. The third day I was away, my daughter called at 6 a.m. to say Nelson was dead. He'd had*

> *a heart attack outside Woolworth's and fell on the sidewalk. By the time an ambulance arrived, he was dead. Just like that.*
>
> *The funeral was a nightmare for me. I don't know how I survived it. I said all the right things, you follow me? But I hated the son of a bitch so strongly that I had to bite my tongue.*
>
> *I've been to visit his grave once because my daughter wanted to go and she was driving. I wouldn't walk around the corner to see him.*
>
> *I could never get over Emma and her feeling. It was the darndest thing.*

A husband's death certificate may be considered a wife's Emancipation Proclamation. But while the gates of the institution stand wide open at last, the released inmate is afraid to budge. The trouble is, there's no place to go. Becky experienced anger, fear, and paralysis:

> *I felt two things: impatience to get the burial over with and anger at him for dying and leaving me alone. I couldn't imagine life without him. I had no life without him. I'd never been trained to do anything. All I knew was taking care of him and the children. Now that I suddenly had nobody to look after, it terrified me.*
>
> *Sally said, "Mommy, you can do whatever you want now." It turned out he was better insured than I knew. But what difference did it make?*
>
> *There was nothing I wanted to do.*

II. LIBERATION

Elegies to His Memory. Baby truly has come a long way. But after seven decades of pretending she's a mini-person who forever needs protection and supervision, liberation is difficult to welcome. So deeply ingrained may be the mannerisms of Daddy's darling little girl, the coy bundle of sweetness who captures a man's heart with beauty, smiles, and obedience, that sometimes she's incapable of discarding a lifelong habit. Then she looks for other protectors.

What's surprising, however, is that so many widows do manage to ditch Little Darling, and, for the first time, live hearty independent lives without pretense or political folderol. Since she has outdistanced the male power structure, there is no further need to impersonate a bimbo. She can be, and usually is, as strong, bitchy, and selfish as she pleases. Each morning she awakes with a heavenly thought: She doesn't have to do a damn thing she doesn't want.

The elderly woman is the freest woman of all, simply because she has outlasted the landmarks of her life: Daddy, boyfriends and lovers, teachers and bosses, Daddy's stand-in—her husband. No man wants to own her now. No man cares enough to boss her. If that means loneliness, it is also her liberation.

When she speaks of the men who defined her existence, the men she loved, fed, nagged, nursed, and obeyed, her songs of mourning are neither sentimental nor particularly gracious. Pearl pays her respects to two husbands:

> *My first husband, Johnny, was a house painter. He got himself killed in '39 by falling off the roof of the Methodist Church. I was married to him about ten years but it's been a long time now. I do remember he used to drink pretty bad. He'd get into some awful brawls down at the bar. I knew better than to fuss with him then. I'd run out the back door and over to my sister's. When he'd sober up, he used to come bring me home. After I had two babies to tend, it was harder to run. I'd lock myself in the bathroom.*
>
> *I married right after high school. June 15. Johnny was handsome. He had shiny black hair and black eyes and beautiful olive skin. He was what they call "a ladies' man." He was always looking. That's*

what I hated about him. Even if I was beside him, he couldn't walk down the street without looking at every woman he passed. He acted as though I wasn't there. I don't think he knew how much he hurt me.

It nearly broke my heart the first time I found out he was unfaithful with a seventeen-year-old girl from the post office. I went to my sister's and cried for two days. Josie said, "You stay here awhile and make him feel real ashamed and then you go back." I told her I was never going back. She said, "Honey, you're crazy. What're you going to live on? Your looks?" I went home.

I don't remember what I felt when he died. Nothing much, I guess. Now that I think about it, though, I guess it was the best thing that could have happened. He was getting to be a mean bastard and most likely he would have turned meaner.

With the insurance he left and living at my sister's, I got by. Then the war started and I got a job at the Armco plant. Billy and Jimmy were almost teen-agers. Those were good years, maybe the best. I had plenty of money, plenty of pretty clothes, and I had a wash-and-set every Saturday. There was nobody telling me what to do. I did as I pleased and raised my sons to be fine boys. Every August we'd go to Atlantic City for two weeks with my sister and brother-in-law and their kids. I had a couple of boyfriends but the big thing in my life was dancing. I was crazy about dancing and I only cared that men be good dancers. Josie said, "You should think about getting married again." I told her, "It's too much fun being a widow." And, you know, that was the God's truth.

After the war it was hard to find work. I was about thirty-five then, too old for dancing and partying and carrying on. When Mr. Gallagher asked me to marry him I didn't stop to think. I

> *said, "Yes." He was a man and a teetotaler and he owned two filling stations and a black Hudson. Mr. Gallagher was a widower. He had one daughter who lived in Louisville. Listen, I just wish I could have had a seance or something and talked to his wife. Mr. Gallagher said she died of cancer but I never believed it. He nagged her to death.*
>
> *His first name was Owen. When we were alone, he allowed me to call him Owen but around people I had to say Mister. I'd phone Josie and say, real sarcastic, "Mister Gallagher says it's going to snow today." And we'd laugh and laugh.*
>
> *Oh, he was a tight son of a bitch! I had to account for every penny and then some. Once I threw away a sterling knife by accident. I must have dumped it out with the garbage. For ten years afterward, he was still throwing it up to me.*
>
> *He was always nagging and yelling and bossing and fussing. Nothing I did suited him. He was always correcting me; he always knew better, always had to have the first word and the last. If I disagreed with him, he'd say, "None of your lip now."*
>
> *Many, many times I thought about leaving him or poisoning him. I wonder how I stood him for twenty years. Later on he had prostate trouble. In '60 he had a bad spell but he recovered. When I got to feeling real poorly, I'd tell myself, "This can't last forever."*
>
> *He died in '64.*

A summer vacation forty years ago remains memorable for a small victory. Irene resurrects a husband and a lover, both now dead:

> *The summer of 1933 we rented a house on Cape Cod near Truro. Alan would spend two or three weeks at a time with me and the children and then go back to the city for a week or so to look after his business.*

> *I met a painter who was rather well-known at the time. I fell in love with him and soon we began to sleep together when my husband was in town. Since everyone in the community knew each other, I couldn't hide knowing Patrick. I invited him to the house and he and my husband became friends.*
>
> *I think my greatest kick was that summer when I slept with two men at the same time. I felt so clever because my husband thought I was incapable of doing anything like that. I remember very clearly him saying to me once, "You could never be unfaithful. You're not made like that." And I thought to myself, "Oh, yes I am."*
>
> *In September when we were going home, Patrick gave me a painting. I was thrilled—it was worth a thousand dollars—and hung it in the living room. Whenever guests came to the house, Alan would proudly call their attention to the picture and he never failed to mention it was a gift to me from Patrick. I don't believe the obvious ever occurred to him: that the painting wasn't free. He always assumed I was true blue, a totally devoted wife.*
>
> *I had a good time in bed with both of them but the real pleasure came from knowing I was tricking my husband.*

Becky furnishes a somber retrospective of the two most important men in her life, Daddy and her husband Max:

> *My father was the kind of person who kept you at arm's length. He didn't show a lot of affection. When I'd ask my mother if he loved me, she'd say, "He thinks a lot of you, Becky." He was affectionate when he thought about it but he didn't think about it often. I guess he did love me. He just didn't show it.*
>
> *My husband was the same way. Max knew nothing about me. For thirty-five years, he'd say,*

"Becky, I'll never understand you." His picture of me was terribly, terribly distorted. I came into focus for him at certain times: when we were making love, when the children were born, when he was eating one of his favorite dishes. He loved my potato salad. Or when we had a fight. The rest of the time I could have been anyone.

I lived a life he knew nothing about.

If I Had My Life to Live Over. One might think that a woman who has spent forty or fifty years bending over children and husband would have difficulty standing upright, let alone be able to furnish a manifesto for revolution. And yet her examination of the life she led in a man's world cannot help but reveal the answer to "What do women want?" It is simply this: If she could live her life over, she would live it to suit herself.

Looking back, she feels no qualms about thumbing her nose at woman's place, including the babies and husbands who kept her nicely fastened there. For she spent her life gazing thirstily at the horizon. What lay beyond it, she could only read about. The public libraries are supported by women living men's lives to the fullest.

If she had been able to chart her own course, where would she have sailed? Away, she says, far away. Nearly always her destination—Paris, the seashore, Africa—turns out to fall into the category of cliche. It is no place Ernest Hemingway and her *National Geographic* subscription haven't covered in loving detail.

And what will she do when she arrives? How will she live? She can barely say. Getting there exhausts her imagination.

Four women sail their memories in a quest for what might have been:

RUTH - I had five children but my little boy Sammie died when he was three. They are good children, all of them. They write me regularly, except Janie.

She's always been bad about letters. I worry about my kids but their lives are none of my business now. I don't ask questions. I don't give advice.

Sometimes I think I would have been happier if I hadn't had children. When I think back, I see there was so much pain on their account. They put a fence around my life.

I never thought about what it would mean to have kids. I just had them. Two months after I married, I got pregnant. All through my twenties it seems like I was expecting. That part of my life was one long pregnancy. I never went anywhere. Then there was no such thing as babysitters. If you wanted to go somewhere, you asked your mother or your mother-in-law to look after the kids. Later on the oldest looked after the young ones. On Sundays I would fry chicken and fill a thermos with iced tea and we'd drive some place, usually to the state park or to Uncle Dan's.

It's hard to imagine my life without children but I believe it would have been happy. I'm sure I would have left New York. I always wanted to live in Paris and sit in a sidewalk cafe and drink absinthe or whatever people drink there. I'd live in a room or a little apartment without a kitchen. When I felt hungry, I would go to a cafe to eat or buy fruit and rolls. I wouldn't even cook for myself.

I'd only have lovers, many lovers. A husband? Possibly. But no children. I could have lived without them and had a fine life.

PEARL - *I've never felt helpless. I don't sit around all day and watch television like people I know. My life is very full. I have lots of fun with my grands and my church work and my garden. On Saturdays I make me a few dollars helping out down at the beauty shop. I take out rollers and clean up. And I have many friends. I'm happy with my life.*

Would I like to remarry? No, I don't think so. I used to believe it's better to be married. A widow doesn't get so many invitations. People don't want to invite her by herself. But now it doesn't make any difference to me. My friends are nearly all widows, too.

All my life I did for men. Enough is enough. Now I do for me. And my children and grandchildren.

If I were seventeen again, I wouldn't marry right off. I'd prefer to have boyfriends. I'd find myself a nice job. It wouldn't have to pay a lot of money, just enough so I could have a little house and take a nice trip to the seashore every summer. I would have liked to have been a teacher because they don't work in the summers. Then, when I was thirty or thirty-five if there was a man I loved, then maybe I'd get married. But I wouldn't leave my house; I'd make him move in with me. That way, if he got ornery, I could kick him out. I'd say, "This is my house. You be nice to me or you get your ass out."

The trouble with being married was, I felt the house didn't belong to me. The only times I've felt really at home was when I was a little girl back home. And now. To me, it's a good feeling to know you have a home that's yours.

NELLIE - *As a girl I wanted to be somebody: a famous actress or a dancer or a poet. I had so many dreams. I wanted to bloom and express myself and say, "Here I am. Here is what I think and feel. Take me or leave me." I don't recall thinking of those dreams until many years afterward when my husband died. But by that time, I was too old. The future was behind me.*

I met Louis at a Fourth of July picnic. My mother couldn't stand him. When he came to call, she wouldn't say a word to him. Father thought Louis was steady. "A good man," he used to call him, "a good man." Mother never discouraged me from marrying. All she said was, "You're grown-up now. You have to stop your daydreaming." We married a few days before my seventeenth birthday and moved to Denver.

Louis was a quiet, gentle man until something riled him and then he was uncontrollable. He'd hit me or hit one of the children. "He doesn't mean it," I'd tell them. "He's tired." It didn't happen very often. I had a good marriage.

Something I've always wanted to do is travel. I never knew where. Anywhere. It didn't matter. Louis liked to tease me because I was always bringing home piles of books from the library: travel books about Africa and India and islands in the Pacific. My taste was kind of exotic. He ordered me a subscription to National Geographic. I'd read each copy from cover to cover and then start over. It's hard to explain but I always felt a strong desire to ... go. Always I imagined going by myself. Sometimes one of my children would be included by mostly I saw myself alone. Far away. I found those daydreams delicious because they were so peaceful. They comforted me.

GERTRUDE - *When I was a little girl, I loved reading stories about the sea. I'd never seen the ocean or a ship—we lived in West Virginia then—but I knew just what they looked and smelled like. I told my Daddy, "When I grow up, I'm going to work on a ship. I'll sail away to Africa and Spain but I'll bring you back presents from every place I've been."*

I remember feeling angry because he laughed at me: "Ladies don't work on ships. Besides, don't you know it's bad luck to have a woman aboard a ship?" I couldn't understand why women should

> *be bad luck. It didn't make sense. From then on he teased me. "Little sailor lady," he'd call me.*
>
> *I was always a bit of a nut because I remember the things I wanted to be when I grew up and all of them were crazy. For a short time, my ambition was to be a railroad conductor and then a detective and then a newspaper reporter. But I got married.*
>
> *What has bothered me is that everything exciting was off-limits. It was like window-shopping, strolling by and looking and your mouth watering but you could never stop and buy anything.*
>
> *Oftentimes I think my whole life has been spent just passing by.*

In the end, a woman's bitching simply has been a furious cry of Swindle! Little Darling's epitaph can only be this:

PEACE ON EARTH, GOODWILL
TO MEN .... SOMEDAY

About the Author

Marion Meade studied at Northwestern University in Illinois and later received a master's from Columbia Graduate School of Journalism. She worked as a freelance writer and her articles have appeared in leading magazines and newspapers, including the *New York Times*, *McCall's*, the *Village Voice*, *Ms. Magazine*, and *Cosmopolitan*. Meade has written novels, biographies, and nonfiction books. *Bitching* was a significant contribution to the second phase of development in the feminist movement. She has written biographies of Victoria Woodhull (*Free Woman*), Eleanor of Aquitaine, Madame Blavatsky, Buster Keaton (*Cut to the Chase*), Woody Allen (*The Unruly Life of Woody Allen*), and Dorothy Parker (*What Fresh Hell Is This?*). She has published two historical novels: *Sybille*, which narrates the life of a woman troubadour in thirteenth century southern France, during Europe's first great holocaust, the Albigensian crusade; and *Stealing Heaven, The Love Story of Heloise and Abelard*. She lives in New York City.

www.ingramcontent.com/pod-product-compliance
Lightning Source LLC
Chambersburg PA
CBHW031504270326
41930CB00006B/241
* 9 7 8 1 4 9 7 6 3 8 9 7 6 *